This is the story of Toby Thunder's time
as CEO of Eternal Energies (Guildford) Ltd.,
and what happened to him there.

CONTENTS

PREFACE

You are probably looking at this book because you are interested in leadership and are, in all likelihood, in a leadership position of some sort. You will recognise that being a good leader is a constant challenge, and something that remains with you all the time you are with the people you are trying to lead. It is not something that you do intermittently or on a whim. It is also very personal, in that the way one person is effective as a leader, does not necessarily work for someone else. This is particularly true if leadership is an interplay between a person's personality and outlook, the context within which they are working, and their skills and capabilities. The combinations are almost infinite. Look at the differences between all the high-profile effective leaders you can think of.

However, we all have a shadow-side, where we do things that are not so effective, or even have negative impacts on our ability to provide good leadership. I know I have, and so did Churchill and Nelson Mandela to name but two! And that is why this book has been written. The more that you can be aware of your shadow-self, so that you can reduce the negative impact, the better a leader you will be.

The story of Toby Thunder is based on nearly forty years of working with people in leadership positions across a vast variety of organisations. During that time, people have exhibited, described, discussed, and recognised their faults and foibles, as well as the tremendous strengths that they have used as a force for good. The most common theme has been that when you have a worthwhile purpose that you pursue in your work, it makes providing good leadership so much easier. The events depicted in the book are therefore a compendium of situations that have all actually occurred. Nothing has been made up, although some events have been embellished for dramatic effect. Many of them I have seen first-hand, while others have been revealed in coaching conversations or small group discussions.

The events have been presented to be read in the same way one might read an Aesop Fable. In other words, any moral or learning that may be gleaned is not spelt out. What might be a lesson for one person, may be a different lesson for another. It is therefore up to the reader to decide what they take from any part of the book, rather than for me to tell you what you should think. There are too many people that think they have *the* answer.

And if we are talking about sins, why not focus on the traditional seven? After all, many others before me have. The answer is, of course, that in terms of leadership, there are way more than seven. Your challenge is to see how many make sense to you, and how many of them apply to you. Your next challenge is to work out what other sins you might have committed that have not been illustrated in the book.

Whether you get to the end or not, can I encourage you to have a look through the Epilogue?

I hope you enjoy the story, and that if nothing else, it makes you think.

1

AT THE END

Toby Thunder reached over his shoulder and painfully extracted the knife that was firmly embedded in his back. The pain was excruciating and the knife metaphorical, but that didn't make it any easier to bear. After scarcely a year into the job of CEO at Eternal Energies, the chairman had just informed him of the board's decision to exercise the escape clause in his contract, and sack him. No pay-off; no compromise or settlement agreement, no thanks, just a cursory,

"I'm sorry, Toby, but it just wasn't going to work."

He'd been at the office for two hours when Annabel, his PA, poked her head around the door and informed him that the chairman would appreciate a word.

"Tell him I'll be along in half-an-hour. But politely of course."

"I got the impression that it was a bit urgent and that you were needed now," she had replied.

Reluctantly, he stopped looking at the not-too-encouraging sales figures, and thinking about what opportunities there might be to improve them, put on his Huntsman jacket, and picked up his phone. He appreciated the fine cut of his Saville Row suit as he passed the mirror behind his PA's desk. One needed to dress to suit one's position. He smiled to himself as he inwardly intoned 'a suit-to-suit sir…' He noted the two security men from the team that served the whole industrial estate where they were based, standing on the other side of the office, as he knocked on the door to the chairman's office, and waited.

More office security measures, he thought to himself. Probably here to conduct another 'constant vigilance' session for the staff. Very Harry Potter. At that moment the door opened, and he was ushered into the chairman's rather austere sanctum.

Half-an-hour later, having handed back his car keys, his laptop, his phone, and his credit cards, he was escorted from the building clutching his leather backpack briefcase that now contained just a few personal effects. Pausing by the designated parking slot and the car he had considered his own, even though it wasn't a marque of his choice, the security men opened the boot, and signalled that he should remove his golf clubs. Looking in the front, he could see the mobile phone holder he'd bought, and a small handful of change.

"I'll take the phone holder," he said, and then rather abruptly, "but keep the change." In fact, he'd have rather liked the change, but felt far too embarrassed to ask for it.

Standing waiting for the taxi, acutely aware that he was in the direct line of sight of the young but competent and attractive receptionist he'd bantered with every morning, he retraced his exit from the building. To be honest, he hadn't seen this coming, in spite of what his wife, Sally, had been saying. And then, as his mind raced, he wondered how easy it was going to be to get another job. Lord knows what sort of reference he'd get from Eternal or his previous position, which had not ended on particularly good terms either. He could feel his confidence deserting him as he recalled the chairman's parting shot,

"We made a mistake, Toby. We thought you had more leadership qualities than you did. You just weren't up to the job."

He had suddenly felt as if he was back at school, facing the rather bullish rugby master who had put him in as captain when the regular captain was attending an interview for a place at Cambridge. The game had been a shambles, as the opposition had run rings around them. But worse had been the moment his shorts had been ripped off, revealing his favourite Star Wars underpants.

"I think the team needed an example to follow rather than avoid," the teacher had remarked afterwards. "A true captain would have encouraged the rest to try harder. Shame! I thought there was more to you. Not a mistake I'll make again."

Crushed, Toby had given up rugby soon after. And then the pain between his shoulder blades returned as he remembered another of the chairman's comments,

"The writing was on the wall the moment you lost the confidence of the staff."

What had made it worse was that two of the senior team were his appointments. He suddenly felt sympathy for all those football managers summarily dismissed that he'd thought of as useless.

As he stood waiting for the taxi, he unconsciously searched for his phone, until he remembered that he no longer had one. Luckily, he had his backpack and golf clubs to hold on to. At least there was one blessing, he hadn't had to leave clutching the seemingly-obligatory cardboard box you so often see staff that have been laid off holding having cleared their office or desk. Returning to his contemplations, he re-lived the walk from the chairman's office. On his way out of the building he could feel eyes following him. He remembered the comment from the operations manager, one of his first appointments, as he looked up from his desk as they passed,

"I'm sure you'll thank us for this one day, Toby. It's got to be for the best all round."

Why might this be 'best' for me, Toby wondered. And, was he imagining it, or had he detected a sense of relief from behind him as Fred and Bobby, the two security staff, guided him across the offices, down the stairs, and back through the preparation and packing rooms to the car park, where they had invited him to retrieve his golf clubs? They couldn't have made it more humiliating if they'd tried.

The taxi arrived and he clambered into the back. He gave the driver his home address, and realised that he was hugging his golf clubs rather too tightly for comfort. Moving them into the other footwell, he hoped the driver hadn't noticed and thought him odd or weak in some way.

"Taking the day off for a game of golf? Wish I had that luxury. Come to think of it, I wish I could play golf! Love watching it, just can't play," the driver chortled.

With some relief, Toby answered, "Something like that."

"So, have you got a handicap then?"

Toby pondered this for a short while. Yes, he played off a 10, which was above average for men, but his mind wandered to other interpretations of the term. Was there something about him that made it difficult to be an effective leader? Was he 'handicapped' in some way? And if so, why had it suddenly appeared now? He had been very good in his previous roles. Everyone had said so, and the results were not bad either.

At that moment, they passed a church with a poster outside declaring that '*The wages of sin are death, the gift of God is eternal life*'. Ironic that the company he had just left was Eternal Energies, but more thought provokingly, had he committed any leadership 'sins' that had led to his 'death' as their CEO? What was there he could not see? Returning to the idea of a handicap, he began to think about what his failings might have been. He had tried his best, worked hard, and had been focused on delivering the results he had been employed to deliver. He'd had some positive feedback about his presentations and had good relations with most of the staff, with one or two notable exceptions. The idea of some deadly sins of leadership rang a bell for him, but from where he could not recall. As his mind wandered, he was brought back to earth again by the taxi driver,

"I meant a golf handicap," explained the driver embarrassedly, clearly under the impression that he'd just insulted his passenger given the silence.

"Sorry, mate, miles away," replied Toby. "I play off a 10 normally, but haven't really had much time for golf recently. Very busy at work."

"So, what do you do at Eternal then?" asked the driver.

Toby suddenly found himself unable to decide how to answer. He couldn't admit he'd just been summarily dismissed, but equally, he could no longer claim to be CEO. Perhaps he should claim to be off on holiday? Then his dilemma disappeared as his anger suddenly boiled to the surface,

"I had a management role, but I don't think I'll be with them for much longer. In fact, this might be my last day! Bit too toxic of an environment for me. There are better ways to spend your life than trying to get incompetent people to do a decent job, and senior people to raise their eyes from the feeding trough."

"I'd heard that it wasn't such a happy ship these days," replied the driver. "Better off out of it if you ask me."

"Perhaps," Toby said quietly, and drifted back to his own thoughts.

His heart sank as he thought about the look his wife would surely give him as she went on about the things he should have done differently, and her warnings that he had ignored. She'd been cautioning him for weeks that he needed to be careful, but he'd always thought that she was misreading the situations he reported. Surely it would be difficult for her to see the complexities of the business, and what leadership and management was about? In fact, he now regretted the way he had felt the need to patiently explain that these sorts of things were 'business-as-usual' in the cut and thrust of the modern business world; a world she had not inhabited for quite some time. True, she'd had a corporate job before they had children, but Human Resources always seemed slightly out of touch with the realities of business. Now that she volunteered at the Citizens Advice Bureau, with three shifts at the local library, she must be well out of touch.

Worse still was the derision he would receive from his son, no doubt wearing one of his many black tee-shirts with 'anti-this' and 'anti-that' slogans. Now there was someone that could benefit from some corporate exposure. He should surely be bright enough to do well in a bank or IT company, having a first in Maths from Newcastle, but what good was an internship with the World Wildlife Fund going to do him? Where was the value in that? And they had bonded so well when he was younger; many a happy weekend had been spent watching or playing football, or following Formula One on the television.

Glancing at the dashboard and wondering what sort of car he was in, he noticed the meter clocking up the fare. Panicking, he realised that he wasn't sure if he had enough money to pay for the ride. Feeling for the wallet in his backpack, he retrieved it and found that he had £25 in cash, a multitude of loyalty cards, a few receipts, his driving licence (with the wrong address – not a good look), two out-of-date credit cards, and the joint bank account debit card.

"Can I pay by card?" Toby asked.

"Normally, yes. But I can't guarantee it as the service has been very on/off the past week. Is that a problem? Our office would have mentioned it when you booked the ride."

"Unfortunately, I didn't make the booking myself. We should be fine," replied Toby.

He couldn't even phone ahead to see if there was money in the housekeeping jar, especially as the gardener and cleaner were due early today, and hopefully hadn't syphoned it all off. Now there were luxuries they'd have to do without from now on. Well, at least till he got another job. His anxiety began to rise again as he imagined arriving home and there being no cash around to pay the taxi. He began to physically feel an onrush of embarrassment about how it would look. Thinking more widely, he recognised that there were no neighbours he knew well enough to borrow some cash from either, even if they had any. His son was away interrailing for a few months before he started his internship, having already had a year off before going to university in Newcastle, and his daughter was now at university herself. Alright for some, he thought.

Looking out of the window, he spotted a building that used to be his bank. What remained was a cash machine - worries over. The taxi circled slowly around the green in the middle of the picturesque square and back out along the small high street to the ATM. Toby hopped out and just managed to get the PIN right on the third attempt. Checking the balance, he was horrified to see the joint account overdrawn.

"Not another cash-flow crisis," he muttered out loud, before realising he was now at the head of a small queue. Still a cash economy here, he mused. He could get £50 before the overdraft limit was breached, which he wasn't about to do. Sally would give him hell if he created another £75 unauthorised overdraft fee while knowing that there was only one more salary cheque to come.

He pressed the £50 button, and a message flashed up saying that the machine was only dispensing £20 notes at the moment. Cursing to himself, he reduced his withdrawal to £40. Turning, he found himself facing a small queue of people, all looking slightly annoyed, with one pointedly looking at their watch. Trying not to make eye contact, he quickly walked off. Middle England at its worst, he thought to himself.

Returning to the taxi, he changed his mind about going home, and paid the driver off. After all, there was only another three miles to go before he reached home. That left the £40 in his wallet and, as it was a sunny morning, he shouldered his golf clubs and wandered down to the pub by the river. It was a popular haunt for many due to the beautiful setting and half-decent food. It was only 11.45 am, but he felt he'd already done a day's work and needed a bit of down time. He was still feeling shell-shocked, so perhaps a drink and a quiet sit would help him sort things out. As an introvert,[1] some time on his own to work through things suited him well. And a pint of Old Speckled Hen, a hot sausage sandwich, and a bag of cheese and onion crisps certainly wouldn't go amiss.

Toby settled himself into a chair to wait for his sandwich as the kitchens had only just got going again after breakfast, and looked out over the river. His eyes drifted to the swans serenely floating on the river, and he imagined their feet madly paddling under the surface.

A suitable metaphor for my time at Eternal Energies, he thought, and began to go over what had happened.

---

[1] For anyone familiar with Myers Briggs, his Type Indicator was ISFJ.

2

IN THE BEGINNING...

It all began when a head-hunter had contacted him at his previous employer. He had been Commercial Director there with P&L responsibility for over £1.5 million worth of product. Having come up through the sales function of several previous organisations, then into key account management, and finally business development, he had been perfectly placed for this broader commercial role overseeing sales, marketing, and customer service functions. The business had done well, and even in the dark years following the banking crisis, had managed to be commercially successful. This was in large part due to Toby's ability to build harmonious teams, and his skills in managing larger accounts where he usually developed good relationships with key people.

The Toby that was head-hunted for the role at Eternal Energies, however, had only really emerged after he left college and got his first proper job. Prior to that, he had been dogged by a difficult childhood and an even more difficult school experience. His parents had had high expectations of all three of their children. His older brother had flourished at school and did his first degree at St Andrews University, followed by a PhD in Anthropology at Cambridge. He was now an academic, working his way up the university hierarchy at Durham.

With both parents having been teachers, he was considered a success. His younger sister, on whom both parents doted, had gone to art school against their parents' wishes. There, she had met a handsome New Zealander, dropped out, gone travelling, and settled down in New Zealand with two children, all in very quick succession. She had once told Toby that it was as far away as she could get from their parents, having felt suffocated by them throughout her childhood.

Toby, however, felt that he was never in a position to escape the expectations of his parents. His brother was constantly praised for his achievements, and his sister was consistently forgiven for her misdemeanours. That, however, had not stopped his parents arguing about her, her choices, and Toby's own performance - both at school and in sport. His father was more forgiving of his daughter than he was of Toby. His mother was the opposite. Sometimes they rowed quite late into the night, which spilled over into other activities. He inwardly shuddered as he remembered the discomfort of the atmosphere their arguments created, and his desire for something more non-confrontational.

Attending the local grammar school had been difficult too, as his brother had set higher standards than Toby was able to meet. He had been top of his class several times, and successfully captained the rugby and cricket teams. Toby's teachers were constantly indicating that he 'could do better.' In many ways, he had felt belittled by both teachers and fellow pupils. As an example,

Toby had somehow got the nickname 'Poxy,' derived from a geography teacher who had been talking about weather patterns. When he'd talked about storms, he'd mentioned thunder claps, and laughed as he made the connection with Toby's surname. The other kids had quickly caught on, teasing him about whether he had 'the clap,' which mutated into 'the pox,' and then 'Poxy.' The experiences had left him with a lack of confidence and a feeling of inferiority. He had been glad to leave and go to a university where no-one knew him.

With mediocre A Levels, he had just scraped a place at Birmingham City University for an economics degree. There, he drank his way through the three-year programme, but emerged with a half-decent degree. However, to fund the extravagances of a very enjoyable night life, it was there he had discovered his natural talent for selling. Walking through the Birmingham City Centre Bull Ring market one day, he had got into a conversation with a Bangladeshi trader, Imran, who was selling fashion cotton goods he imported directly from family back home. Toby liked his stuff, and had returned a couple of times for more items of clothing. It was on one of these occasions that Imran had offered Toby good commission on any clothes he sold amongst his fellow students. By mastering the art of sales rapport in spite of his introversion, he was eventually making sufficient income to keep him clubbing for at least a couple of nights each week.

Toby's first job after graduating was in a car showroom. He liked smart cars, and had always preferred Formula One (or F1, about which he was quite knowledgeable) to the rugby or cricket he had left behind at school. His apparent natural charm and humour (a defence mechanism developed at school), plus an eye for a sale, enabled him to do well. Over the next few years, he sold computers, photocopiers, and electrical office equipment such as cables, lighting, modems, and monitors, before ending up in the solar generation industry as Commercial Director of a small solar panel import and distribution business.

In one of his jobs, he had met Sally, who had worked her way up from being a receptionist to a CIPD qualified human resources manager. Although he no longer spent his weekends clubbing, he still enjoyed a party, but had also taken up golf as an essential adjunct to his commercial roles. Sally, too, enjoyed a party and F1, and had experimented with golf. Essentially, they were (almost) a match made in heaven. Indeed, in spite of their differences about Toby's work, they still enjoyed each other's company, with many interests and values in common. Within three years of getting married, they had two children, a boy and a girl, and Sally had reduced her workload to look after the children; she had very much enjoyed being 'a mum.' Luckily, this also complimented the relocations Toby's jobs demanded.

More recently, Toby had studied for a part-time MBA at a Birmingham college. The attractions were that it was his old stomping ground, but also one of the least expensive. He felt it had given him a lot of useful tips and techniques. It had also helped him recognise that he perhaps needed to lift his eyes towards the horizon a bit more, and think more holistically about markets and commercial opportunities. It had also helped him hone his analytical skills. On the other hand, he knew that his survival depended on him making his budgets.

Being head-hunted is always flattering, so Toby had decided that he'd show an interest, and see whether the job looked promising. Over the years, he had attended a number of interviews with head-hunters and had completed various psychometrics. It was by now a familiar process, and one he felt he knew how to manage. By this time, Toby had evolved from the night-clubbing student/car salesman, into a much more relaxed and presentable individual. At 6 feet tall and in a well-cut suit, he was a commanding figure. He had learned to look calm, even in the face of adversity, and allow his charm to pilot him through most situations. Having had a career in sales, he maintained an optimism while batting away negative thoughts, convincing himself that success was just around the corner. He was even quite 'good' at psychometrics, having also completed quite a few on his MBA. As such, he had impressed the head-hunters, and was put forward on a short list to the business looking to recruit.

The business turned out to be Eternal Energies (Guildford) Ltd. This was a family-owned business, and it was the first significant external appointment they had made. Up until then, the business had been run by first the founder, and then his son. Other staff were relatives or long-standing employees that had come up through the ranks. Apparently, it was the decision of the son, Hamish, to retire, that had led to the conclusion by the board that bringing in an outsider as CEO would be best for the future of the business. This was particularly the case, as no direct family members were old enough or interested in taking on the role. The only exception to this was Gilbert Turkey, Indirect Sales Manager, who was married to Hamish's daughter. It seemed that there had been some discussion about the problems of her marrying an employee. However, Toby had been told later that none of Eternal Energies' board was prepared to entrust the business to him given his sometimes volatile nature. None of the other senior staff were considered suitable CEO material either. Since he had only learned of this after his appointment, none of this had influenced his decisions, or indeed, would have put him off applying.

The business had been founded by the now deceased Angus Smalley, based on a distribution deal he had made with a German photovoltaic solar panel manufacturer, to which he had added a solar thermal panel, and for which he had developed a small installation team. The company had been one of the first to enter the UK market, and had established a position that other entrants had initially found hard to match. His son Hamish had taken the reins on his father's death ten years previously, and had grown the business using a direct sales force of employees and commission agents. Latterly, he had also appointed a number of intermediaries, and had given the job of managing them to Gilbert, along with direct communications in the form of emails, mail-shots, advertising, and so on. More recently, Hamish had commissioned a website and telephone sales facility. In the end, the website was never developed beyond its initial configuration, and the telephone sales activity was still in the planning stage. Hamish had not been great at following things through.

The panels were prepared at their combined factory and office unit in Guildford. The business employed 30 people, 10 of whom were independent sales operatives. Turnover had grown to £3 million, with a PAT (Profit After Tax, but before dividends) of 10%, which contrasted with a turnover of £1.5 million and PAT of 20% when Hamish had taken over. Although net profits had been reducing as a percentage, the business had always been profitable, with dividends effectively being top-up income for Hamish's sister, dividends for Hamish himself and the Chair, and help with their two children's mortgages and school fees for their offspring. Some more remote family members each held a small number of shares totalling 10% of the shareholding. It had been noted at interview that this income stream, although not great at an individual level, was important for the individuals concerned.

A straightforward family business, nothing strange there, Toby reflected. Why had it become so complicated and difficult to manage? What had he missed?

By the time Toby had joined, the original products were being superseded, as there was a much cheaper array of panels appearing on the market from India and the Far East, plus many more sales, distribution, and installation competitors. Although they had added some to their product range and widened their supply base, the photovoltaic and thermal panels remained a core product for them. To combat the increased level of competition, Hamish had initiated development work on a number of projects to improve sales effectiveness, general efficiency, and reduce costs. He had always believed that they needed to emphasise price in their initial approaches, as this was what was most likely to generate an enquiry.

Gilbert had certainly adopted this philosophy in his communications role, and had got the indirect sales channels to follow a similar path. The business was also searching for another breakthrough technology or product, to supplement the original and current panels that had been so successful for the business. To date, they had added storage batteries and inverters to go with the solar panels, and had begun to wonder whether AI had anything to offer, although any investigation was still in its infancy by the time Hamish had handed in his notice. None of these had, however, yielded significant competitive advantage, as most other suppliers had adopted a similar approach. Toby's mandate had been to lead the company back into a strong competitive position while improving total income for distribution.

Toby had attended an interview twice before the short list was finally reduced to two by Eternal. One meeting had been off-site, with the other on-site on a Sunday, as the board had not wanted to alarm the workforce by telling them the CEO was leaving, and that an unknown would be their new boss. Interviews had been restricted to the chair of the board and an external non-exec. The final interviews were also on-site, but again in secret, and had taken the form of a meeting with the outgoing CEO, the chairman, and then a presentation to the whole board minus the finance director. Toby had wondered about the efficacy of including the departing CEO, but also remembered he was, after all, a shareholder.

The meetings had gone well, and he felt he had made a good impression. He had adhered to the rule of three and had emphasised his previous success; his market analysis, and leadership. He felt they had been interested in his analysis of the market, the trends he had identified, and the opportunities that could be available to take the business to the next level. Solar farms, he felt, were one to be explored, since if they were to only get 1% of the total market, they would instantly treble turnover. There were also opportunities in commercial buildings; E.V. charging, eco-housing, and the potential for recurring revenue from specific app developments. He wondered if a lot of this had been beyond the interviewers' scope or understanding, and whether he had in fact 'blinded them with science.' Nothing extravagant, but giving an image of solidity and confidence in himself which, to be honest, he had genuinely felt.

In terms of leadership, he drew on the books he had read from successful leaders, plus his MBA leadership modules. These had involved a number of case studies, plus some outdoor exercises during the residential weeks. Each exercise had had an appointed leader, who had been required to create a functioning team. He had felt that most of the others were useless. It seemed to him that they issued unclear instructions, indulged in some disparaging remarks about the more hapless members, and had a fundamental misunderstanding of the problems they were trying to solve.

When it had been his turn, he had focused on the small number of competent members, and issued some direct and clear instructions. Although they had all looked a little resentful, he knew that they'd all been grateful to have achieved the task given the fiascos of some of the previous attempts. He felt that he had managed to get through the subsequent feedback session relatively unscathed, and had defended himself quite well, unlike some of his fellow students.

As illustrated in a couple of the books from successful leaders, he had emphasised that leadership was as much about clear direction and resilience, as accommodating people's fragilities and consulting at every step of the way. Often, there simply was not time for this sort of thing, especially when there were budgets to be met. These had been major themes in some of the books he had read, and had worked well with his previous teams. They had always seemed to value his insight and instruction; plus the small adjustments he'd made to their sales pitches to align them with his own approach. When he had asked for feedback, they had always said that they felt he was a good boss! Where one or two had expressed frustration, he had carefully explained to them why he had done or said what he had. They all seemed to understand his points and, as far as he was concerned, went away satisfied. Whenever they got together socially, they had always got on well with no obvious back-biting.

Apart from the importance of having a clear direction, he had also talked about people's need to feel that their leaders had integrity. This was often about being authentic, as well as doing what you say you are going to do. He knew that people needed to feel valued, and that they were clear about their role in achieving the task. Indeed, he had been surprised that the interviewing panel had not heard the anecdote about the floor sweeper at NASA who, on being asked what they were doing, had replied that he was helping put a man on the moon. He also knew from his love of F1, that a clear task and clarity about role were key to improved performance.

In the presentation, he had also used F1 as an example of the importance of feedback. The customer was king in his world, and one needed to listen to them. Well, usually. He described how he was always open to feedback and welcomed any thoughts people had about the best way forward. Businesses such as theirs could no longer rely on the brilliance and drive of one person in this increasingly competitive world. He had hoped that Hamish would notice the implied compliment, and not take it the wrong way.

Looking back, he still believed that he had presented some important points, and genuinely believed that he had tried to embody these principals.

Post interviews and presentations, he remembered almost sabotaging his chances when the non-exec, Burkinshaw, an aging accountant who had worked with the firm for years, approached him over afternoon tea and scones. Having shaken Toby's hand, and possibly held it for slightly longer than was comfortable (Toby had done a meeting, greeting, and hand-shaking course as part of his MBA), Burkenshaw had asked confidentially, "By the way, I was wondering which church you prayed at?"

Toby vaguely remembered that this was often used as a discrete query about people's sexuality. This had completely floored him, as he didn't want to offend, look ignorant, or give the wrong impression in case he was being propositioned. His fears were confirmed when the NED followed up with, "In fact, I was wondering if you knew Dorothy?" another well-known similar question.

"Tricky," he had responded, not quite sure where to go next. "Being married with two children can restrict what one can do," he had eventually answered vaguely.

"No, sure," the NED had replied. "Dorothy is an old friend of the family and is warden at one of the churches near where you live. I just wondered if you'd met her?"

Realising his mistake, Toby had explained, "Yes, I see what you mean. As I said, having two children and always having worked in high pressure jobs, we have very restricted time at weekends, so church isn't something we find easy to fit in." He felt that he couldn't admit that both he and his wife were confirmed non-church people. Moving swiftly on, he had asked, "So, what's your thoughts about how the business might get the growth the board requires?"

"Oh, I don't know," the NED had replied distantly. "I deal with the trusts and wills mostly, although I'm not quite as up-to-date as I used to be. So many more rules and regulations to get to grips with. Still, I think I've kept most things in order. Had a lot of help from Paul Travers. I've been with the business almost since Angus Smalley set it up; good man. And Hamish certainly threw himself into the role when he took over. Shame the profits didn't grow in line with turnover, but I understand the market has become more difficult. Still, I like the business. Edith Smalley, don't think you've met her yet – office manager now, was nanny for Angus's, Hamish's and my children when they were growing up. A bit single minded at times, but very loyal to the company. You should get to know her, can be quite a voice for the family even though she's only a cousin of some sort," and then leaning in more confidentially, "but they do value my opinion when it comes to judging people. I'm sure someone like you is just what the company needs!"

Toby recalled his total excitement the day the chairman had phoned to offer him the job. After initially accepting, he'd then had to backtrack and say that he needed to discuss it with his wife before confirming. He remembered the chairman responding with what Toby thought was an improper remark,

"Well, make up your mind. We didn't come to this decision lightly. Either you want to join us or you don't. Or are you not your own man? We want someone that can get on with things and lead the business, not someone that has to seek approval for their actions."

He had had to bluster a bit at that point. "I'm sure it won't be a problem, but as I'm sure you can appreciate, it's only polite to consult with the other half. Please do go ahead and send through the paperwork."

He also realised at that point that he'd missed the opportunity to negotiate better terms, or enquire about money available for investment. He had kicked himself for being so eager. He'd always been very motivated by reaching the conclusion of 'a deal,' be it a sale, a job, or a purchase. It had been one of his key strengths. Typical, though, to be overcome by the excitement of the moment - he'd done the same thing when offered the commercial directorship!

It had taken three months to complete the transfer to Eternal Energies, as his previous company had not been too pleased when he announced his rather splendid news. As a solar energy company themselves, they had been concerned about the potential for a conflict of interest.

"I don't think that will be a problem," Toby had confided. "They are an occasional customer and not competitors. Remember, I've been here for five years in sales and now done a year as commercial director. I hope you think I've served you well, and wouldn't want to do anything to compromise either you or my new outfit."

"I'm sure you're a man of integrity, Toby," the MD had responded. "But you have to look at it from our point of view. You were not the only internal candidate for the director role, and your departure will raise questions in people's minds about why you are leaving after such a short time. You must have thought of that before you pursued this new opportunity. Don't get me wrong, I can see the attraction of a CEO position, but I'm not sure this move will reflect well on you here. Anyway, you're on three months' notice and we're putting you on gardening leave until your contract expires."

"Can't you allow me to leave earlier? It makes things a bit awkward for my new business."

"I'm not sure we want to do you or them any favours at this moment in time. You'll just have to manage the situation. After all, you are going to be a CEO with much wider responsibilities."

With that, Toby had left his previous employer, now wondering if he should have involved the MD earlier or been a bit more collaborative. After all, it wasn't as if he was looking for another job to get a pay rise as many people do. While on gardening leave until he could join Eternal Energies, he had not been idle. There was a backlog of DIY tasks to be addressed, a house move to organise (rental was so much quicker to sort out), a holiday to arrange, and some new golf courses near their new home to explore. He'd also looked more deeply into the market for solar energy, and how he might grow the business. He had begun to feel that the business was trapped 'inside a box' that kept it as a configuration, installation, and third-party supply company. Surely there were more profits to be gained as an energy supplier, perhaps even wind farms? And what about roofing? Solar roof tiles as a substitute for traditional roofing materials were still in their infancy. If they wanted a breakthrough, here was a great opportunity. Much to investigate and some exciting opportunities to think about. Almost a dream position.

Feeling a bit more 'human' after his light lunch, Toby wondered about a second pint and maybe one of the pub's special pasties. In the end, he settled for a half-pint, a slice of cherry pie and a coffee; americano with some hot milk on the side. He reflected on the excitement he still felt for the intriguing possibilities he had explored prior to joining the company. At the same time, he felt the rising tide of frustration at how he felt he had been thwarted at almost every turn, so that not enough had ever come of these opportunities. It was still a bit of a mystery as to why he had been so restricted, given their desire for profitable growth.

3

THE INTRODUCTION TO THE COMPANY

Settling back down with the half-pint and whiskey chaser he'd quickly added to his order to keep him company while he waited for the coffee and dessert (25-minute delay; short staffed in the kitchens, and the pub was now much busier), Toby began to go over his introduction to the company. He was well aware of the importance of first impressions, and was very good at putting people at ease; making them feel listened to and valued. Although there had been hiccups in his introduction, he didn't think this was where his problems had begun.

When the day came to join the business, his wife had driven him in. Waving his wife goodbye, he walked into reception, nonchalantly carrying his leather backpack briefcase. He noted with approval that the receptionist was both cute and well-presented. Good to have something to create a positive first impression, he recalled.

"Good morning, and how may I help you?" the receptionist had asked.

"And good morning to you. Toby Thunder for the chairman, I believe he's expecting me," he replied, giving her his most winning smile.

"Sorry, nothing here about a Toby Thunder. Which company are you from?"

That's a tricky one, Toby mused, "Best put me down as EE," he had replied brightly, pleased with his quick thinking.

"I'm afraid we've already got a phone supplier. Perhaps you'd like to email in and make an appointment with Mr Paul Travers. He's our finance manager, and in charge of that sort of thing."

"Sorry, I didn't mean to confuse you. I'm not here for telephones. The chairman explicitly told me to report to the front desk at nine o'clock, which I presume is you, and he would meet me here, although he didn't mention that it would be such a pleasant experience."

It had always been his practice to engage with receptionists to get them on his side, as the good ones were either effective gatekeepers, or able to point him in the right direction - and even get him in to see the right people sometimes. Flattery was always welcome, he always assumed, and if they were just airheads, it did no harm anyway. He remembered feeling that this might be one of the good ones. Very useful.

"I presume you are referring to the art-work. I'm quite proud of it actually. I was asked to create a welcoming reception area, and I decided some nice paintings plus that piece of sculpture over there might do the job.

Most of them come from people in my evening art class. Glad you appreciate them. I'll let them know. However, if you're not in my book, there's not much I can do for you. We never entertain cold-callers, and you would not believe the number of people that claim the chairman, CEO, or some other manager has asked them to visit. I'm afraid you'll just have to wait over there, but if no-one has come in 30 minutes, I'll have to call Estate Security," she had replied.

"My wife's the art-lover in our family." Toby hoped this might get her more on his side. As he hadn't really noticed the paintings or sculpture, he felt at a loss what to say next. He had been about to try again with a bit more banter, when the chairman appeared to rescue the situation, and escorted him upstairs to his office.

"Nearly didn't get past the receptionist," Toby had joked. "Looks good though."

"Yes, I suppose so," the chairman had replied. "We all thought it wise to keep your arrival under wraps. We haven't officially announced Hamish's departure yet as we didn't want to create any FUD."

Not wanting to show himself up, Toby had airily interjected with, "FUD, just remind me what that stands for. Just can't bring it to mind."

"Of course: Fear, Uncertainty and Doubt, FUD. I learnt a long time ago that missions can be ruined if people get spooked. The plan is to have a town hall meeting of all staff except the SMT; you'll meet them later. I'll make the announcement and then hand over to you; '*fait accompli*'. That will avoid any unnecessary gossip and tittle-tattle. Should be able to get back to work forthwith."

The town hall was scheduled for 9.30. That had given Toby 20 minutes to think about the introductory speech he had prepared, and what he might want to add. The chairman had indicated that Toby should wait in his office until the appointed hour, at which point he would take him downstairs to the loading bay and make the announcements. As he sat in the office, musing at the lack of any pictures or personal effects in stark contrast with the reception area, the term 'Mushroom Management' came to mind. He'd read about it once, so it was interesting to see it in practice.

'Well,' he thought to himself, *'I suspect the business could benefit from a bit more openness and transparency. Maybe I'll make reference to that in my introduction; nail my colours to the mast from the off. People really need to know where I'm coming from if we want to avoid any FUD.'* Toby smiled gently to himself as he practiced saying the term in different ways, as it was obviously part of the language of Eternal's senior management.

Come 9.30, the chairman had returned and indicated that Toby should follow him. Toby had checked him out in an internet search while on gardening leave, and had discovered that he'd spent 20 years in the Royal Signals working on the power supply side before leaving to join first, one of the big power supply companies, then a smaller power company, before taking up a number of NED roles. Eternal Energies was his first role as chair. He recognised the rather clipped, militaristic approach, plus the giveaway tendency to march everywhere. It was not uncommon for senior military personnel to end up on the boards of smaller companies. Something about the military background seemed to provide a bit of comfort for some reason.

"Now listen up, everyone!" the Chairman had begun. "Some of you will be aware that Hamish has had a few health issues lately, and with the board's agreement, he has decided that his time at the helm of Eternal Energies should come to an end. He wanted to spend more time with his family and get himself back to a healthy position. We are all very grateful for his hard work and application in taking the business forward and leaving us is such a great position, but all good things must come to an end sometime." Ignoring the sudden onset of hushed conversations and shocked expressions, he had pressed on, "When we agreed to Hamish's departure, we looked far and wide for a suitable replacement, and have been lucky enough to secure the services of Mr Thunder here. We all know that Hamish's boots will be hard to fill, but we are sure that we have the right man to fill them. We had to keep the change under wraps till now to avoid any adverse reaction from the market or our suppliers, with whom Hamish had some good relationships. I'm sure you will all understand. Anyway, without further ado, I'll let Mr Thunder introduce himself so that you can all get back to work as soon as possible. Carry on."

With that he'd strode off, leaving Toby looking at the assembled staff, and them looking rather curiously, and perhaps apprehensively, at him. He realised that it would be good to find something to stand on, and pulled over a nearby box. This, unfortunately, collapsed, and he was caught by two of the staff that had seen the disaster coming. There were some titters among the assembled workforce, and Toby felt distinctly uncomfortable. He never liked to make a fool of himself, but knew he had to plough on.

"Right," he had started, unable to think of a *bon mot* to reduce the embarrassment of his tumble, "allow me to introduce myself; I'm Toby Thunder, and I apologise for taking everyone by surprise. I hadn't realised that this was going to be breaking news. I've always believed in full disclosure and openness. Anyway, please call me Toby, I don't like standing on ceremony… let alone boxes." At last, something to lighten the mood and raise a few smiles. He recalled noting the atmosphere becoming less tense. Feeling better, he had continued, "Let me start by saying a bit about myself. I am basically a commercial person with a strong sales background. I was commercial director at my last business, which also dealt in solar panels, but not as direct competitors of Eternal. In fact, Eternal was one of our customers. I like to have good relationships with the people that work for me, and I am always interested in other people's opinions. In fact, my door is always open, so long as you don't want to complain… Only joking! Please, feel free to come and talk to me about anything that interests or concerns you." (Had that been a bit too much like a section of his C.V.?)

He then gave his prepared speech, which he hoped would be rousing and inspiring. He explained that he'd only met Hamish on a small number of occasions, but thought he'd clearly been very enterprising for the business, and that he hoped to build on the solid foundations of the company. There were some great opportunities out there, and he fully intended to take advantage of at least some of them. He thought he'd heard a, *'you'll be lucky'* mumble from somewhere, but couldn't be sure. In answer to his, *'any questions?'* he'd had:

"How long has this been going on? What were Hamish's health issues?" and, "What have you been CEO of before?" Again, he thought he'd heard a mumble in answer to the health issues of, *'sclerosis of the liver I suspect,'* which had made him think.

Toby ended by wishing them all well, shaking hands with everyone there, and promising to speak to everyone individually before too long. With that, he made his way back to the chairman's office. Apart from Hamish and the board, the only other person that had met Toby was Annabel, Hamish's PA, whom Toby had agreed to keep. He'd been impressed by her when they'd met, and not just by her striking good looks. Annabel had seen to all the arrangements for Toby's company car, phone, computer, and credit card. Toby had requested a high-end electric car as his vehicle of choice, as this would reflect the company's main focus (and he rather fancied one), but had had to settle for a lesser make. He had, however, managed to persuade Annabel to organise a reserved parking space, given the restricted size of the company car park. No-one else had a reserved spot, but she had managed to get it organised in the absence of any push-back from the departing operations manager. In effect, he was ready to hit the ground running. Following a health and safety briefing, he had been shown to his office, and spent the rest of the day getting to grips with his new computer, the email system, and trying to access the various company documents.

Looking back, he was rather pleased with his address to the staff, in spite of the initial mishap. In retrospect, he should have recognised that the damned box was too flimsy to take his weight, and asked someone to find him something more substantial. Luckily, he'd looked up great speeches on the Internet, and had cobbled together a few of the best bits. He had particularly liked the SAS-based book: 'Who Dares Wins,' and had used the example it provided:

> "*Many failures are possible, likely even, but failure is not something that should stop us pressing forward. If you can get up off the floor, you'll find there are many new opportunities just ahead of you that you can make happen.*"

Inspiring, he had thought when he came across it, especially as it echoed a lot of his experience in sales. Getting up off the floor had also resonated with the unfortunate experience with the overly-flimsy box. To be fair, that *had* caused some amusement but, he hoped, hadn't made him look like a clown. The speech had also included references to integrity, teamwork, respect, and so on, as well as his open-door statement. He hoped his closing message had been understood when he'd made it clear that he expected an honest day's work for an honest day's pay, although the extra mile would always be rewarded. Firm, but fair, he reflected. Given the importance he attached to first impressions, he'd set out to start with a bang, although falling off a box had not been part of the plan! In retrospect, he wondered whether his desire to convey the ideas of an honest day's work, and firm but fair, had needed greater emphasis.

The next day was given over to individual conversations with the small number of senior management team (SMT) members, to find out a little about them. Crucially, he needed to establish their loyalty and support for 'the journey' they were all about to embark upon. When asked about what was at the end of the journey, he had simply said,

"A better world for us all; oh yes, I think we will all be much better off," which had certainly seemed to impress them into silence.

In particular, Gilbert Turkey had reacted with, "Well, it would be great if you can pull that one off!" Toby still thought Turkey was an odd name though.

Over a sandwich and coffee for lunch, provided by Annabel, he thought about the team, and what he might get out of the SMT meeting he'd requested for the following day. He'd been surprised that Annabel had asked if he'd like a 'sharpener' to go with lunch, to set him up for the afternoon. Apparently, it was something that Hamish had instituted, and often shared with his operations manager. This had reminded him of the liver sclerosis comment he thought he'd heard during his town hall presentation, and he wondered whether Hamish had been aware of how much people thought they saw. Somehow or other, staff always seem to see more than you think they do. He'd have to watch his step, he remembered thinking to himself as he refused her offer.

The SMT meeting had been a quiet affair, consisting of Gilbert Turkey (Indirect Sales), Paul Travers (Finance), Ian Long (Sales and Marketing Manager), and Edith Smalley (Office Manager). When Hamish had retired, so had the operations manager. He had been Hamish's right-hand man, but had also had health problems for some time, so Hamish's departure was a good moment for his own retirement. The gap meant that one of Toby's first jobs was to find a replacement to beef up the team. He also wondered if they really needed an office manager, given that there were only four administrative personnel, and some of them were shared with the finance manager.

He'd given an abbreviated version of his address to the staff to the assembled SMT, during which he noted quite a lot of looking out of the window, or phone-scrolling. Not a comfortable memory, and he still wondered what had disengaged them. In the ensuing discussions, he had been pressed on his ideas for the business, and how he might be different from Hamish. As he wasn't sure how Hamish had been, he found this difficult, so he went into 'consultative sales mode,' and tried to work out what they were looking for. After a while, he had formed the distinct impression that Hamish had been a bit of a '*bon viveur*'; charming, loquacious after a drink, good relationships with suppliers, and could be relied upon to work well with wavering customers. However, he had left a lot of unfinished projects, some of which had been hanging around for months, if not a year or so.

He remembered feeling positive, as what they seemed to want were all the things he'd included in his presentations: direction, integrity, fairness etc. So why the apparent disinterest? Hamish, it seemed, had been good at presentations, but poor on delivering the goods. They felt the development of the business had been a bit haphazard, with Hamish frequently changing things at a moment's notice. As a consequence, they had often been unsure about what their priorities were, or what strategy they were following. They were looking forward to a clear strategy from Toby, which he felt confident he could provide.

However, this had also made his initial intentions a little more difficult, as he'd planned for them to carry on as before while he got his feet under the table and homed in on the best opportunities for profitable growth. But as this was the only idea he had had at the time, he'd had to pursue that path, but with promises to present a plan A.S.A.P. Although the meeting had ended well, if not with the high level of engagement he had hoped for, he had also detected a reserve in both Gilbert and Paul. They hadn't said much, but also hadn't been openly hostile; perhaps just a little negative with remarks such as:

"Good to have a bit of new blood in the business. I think we can all agree that we hope you have better luck bringing the board with you. Not easy at times!" And, "Sounds like you know the market well. Let's trust you have better luck squeezing more profit out of it."

On the one hand, their comments had made him wonder whether they would be opportunity-killers. He'd come across people like that in the past, although not as his direct reports. Such people often positioned themselves as 'Devil's Advocates,' so as to avoid responsibility for the views they were promulgating. In the end, the senior person present had usually thanked them for their thoughts and promised to consider the points they had raised, or take them up with someone higher in the organisation. Toby had seen clearly that this was unlikely to be the case, but it had been an expedient way of ignoring them. On the other hand, he now reflected, maybe he'd missed some key messages about what his priorities should have been. Working more closely with the board maybe? Focussing more on profit than growth? All a bit late now!

Returning to his new office and his new PA, Toby sat behind his desk, fired up his laptop, and began to look through the emails that had already begun to arrive. *'Blow me,'* he mused, *'news gets around fast!'*

Many were from people offering all sorts of services, from recruitment to accounting, but which now included the offer of AI-supported output. He wasn't sure about AI being much more a relationships person than a 'techno' sales person. Included were a couple of customer complaints that clearly needed looking into, and he wondered why they had come directly to him. There was also a request from the auditors for some information - that was now two months overdue - that needed to be provided before the end of the following week, or else they wouldn't be able to sign off the accounts.

Just then, Annabel appeared with a cup of tea, and he decided that 'sharpeners' were definitely off the menu given the sharp-eyed nature of the staff. Bad optics, he remembered thinking to himself, still rather enjoying the play on words. He had also started to consider an operations manager, and had immediately thought of Bob Meadows, whom he had known in a previous job. Bob was very competent, and had a reputation for being good with people, and able to deliver efficiency and quality improvements at the same time. He was also experienced in logistics and customer service management. Although fierce, he was straight talking and fair, and Toby hoped he would complement his own positioning as 'firm but fair.' Bob wouldn't come cheap, but Toby reasoned that he would more than earn his corn. Not wishing to hang around, he had decided to see if he could raise him on the phone. He got through almost immediately.

"Bob, Toby Thunder here. Long time, no speak. How are things with you?"

"Not too bad, thanks," Bob had replied. "You know me, trucking along, getting stuff done, fighting the system as usual! How about you?"

"Good, thanks. In fact, very good. Got a new job as CEO of Eternal Energy down here in Guildford. Very exciting. Old family business based around solar energy, but they decided they needed an external appointment when the previous CEO took early retirement. The operations manager went at the same time, so you can probably guess why I'm phoning."

"Okay. Tell me more," returned Bob.

"Well, I was wondering if you'd be interested in joining me here. You know, new challenge, get the old team back together. Take the business to new horizons. Some big opportunities out there just waiting for us to take advantage of them. It's also a doable commute for you if you're still at your old address."

"Sounds intriguing. As you'll recall, if you can deliver, then I can do the business behind the scenes. But you will have to deliver, Toby. How certain are you that you'll be able to deliver? I don't want to be lumbered with another scramble to keep a business afloat. I've got enough of that here."

"Don't you worry about that, old chum," Toby had rejoindered. "There's plenty of meat out there; enough for everyone. We'll only need to take a small percentage of some of the markets to make a massive difference to the business here. Shouldn't be too hard."

"I hope that's not the salesman in you talking, but the CEO. You know how carried away you can get sometimes. Especially when you're on the hunt."

"No, trust me on this one. I've got to deliver profitable growth to the board, and I fully intend to do so. This is probably the job I've been working towards for the past few years, and I don't propose to screw it up. This will be a new beginning for me and should lead to bigger and better things… maybe for both of us." Toby had recognised that he *was*, perhaps, in 'selling' mode, but knew he wanted Bob if at all possible.

"Okay, send me a job description. You know what salary I'll need. I'll get back to you within the next seven days. The HR people here aren't that great; they seem to have me on a two-week notice period, and I'll need a week's break if I come. And frankly, the HR people aren't the only weak link here, so if everything looks okay, I might be able to join you within the month."

Toby had then put together a package he felt would be attractive to Bob, as he really believed he would be a great asset for the business, and remembered feeling very pleased with himself. When Bob accepted, Toby then only needed to get the chairman's approval and agree the salary. In the event, the chairman had expressed surprise at being asked for his endorsement without any prior consultation, plus the size of salary being offered. In retrospect, he wondered if he should have taken more notice of the chairman's comments about consultation?

"You get what you pay for these days. If we want quality, we have to accept that quality costs," had been Toby's justification. "And we need to get on top of operations ASAP; they look a bit rudderless at the moment, so I thought we needed to fast-track a competent person in forthwith."

Although the chairman had been reluctant to agree to the salary Bob would need, in the end he acquiesced, and wished Toby luck with his first recruit, "If you need any support, just let me know," had been his final comment.

Feeling on a roll, and not in need of any support, Toby also took the opportunity to raise another question, "By the way, if we are looking to save money, I'm not sure we need an office manager. There aren't many staff to cover, and most of them are shared with Paul Travers anyway."

Looking distinctly uncomfortable, the chairman had explained, "Look, the truth is that Edith is a Smalley; a *distant* relative, but held in some esteem by the family. Over the years she has provided a lot of childcare. However, being a very minor shareholder, she does need the job to support herself and her cat refuge. Couldn't possibly let her go, there would be a lot of resistance at board-level from Hamish, his sister; as representative of the wider family, and, of course, Mr Burkenshaw, the NED. They are very close."

Feeling slightly frustrated, Toby had left the office: 'jobs for the boys', or in this case, 'girls', was not something he really approved of. However, he recognised that it was often a feature of family businesses. Often to their detriment. At least he could now go back to Bob Meadows and confirm his appointment. As he sat by the river, he enjoyed reliving the feeling of positivity that he had experienced at that moment.

4

THE FIRST 100 DAYS

Toby knew that the first 100 days would be crucial for him. The tone that he established would more than likely make or break his efforts to take the business forward. He had seen other incoming leaders in the businesses he had worked for spend too much time 'assimilating' or indulging in a 'hand-over', after which people had come to the conclusion that the new leader had little to offer. Two times out of three, this had proved to be true.

He had recognised a long time ago that customers were the life-blood of the business. The logic was simple, but too often not acknowledged by other functions within a business. Without customers there was no income, and a downward spiral would ensue. Reduced income would invariably be followed by cuts that further reduced the ability to win customers, and so on. But that raised the question of how to make sure everyone recognised this and adopted a positive 'customer focus'. He had wondered whether he should send an email round; hold another town hall, or rely on the SMT to spread the word? He hadn't quite decided which was best, so he'd put the decision in the 'non-urgent' box to be returned to when he had a better handle on the company as a whole. Looking back, he realised that this had remained in the 'non-urgent' box and never resurrected. Just too busy, he said to himself as he gazed at the swans gracefully moving about on the river.

Given the importance of maintaining and growing income, Toby had concentrated his initial efforts on assessing the sales force. His long experience with direct sales forces had enabled him to understand the quality of the team he had inherited at Eternal. In general, he had not been too impressed. At least six were 'Steady Eddies' that had been with the business a long time, and came with a whiff of the 'double-glazing/time-share' sales methods that had been needed in the early days of solar panels. Added to this, they were expensive. Accordingly, he instituted a no-replacement policy for any direct sales people that retired or moved on, with a view that he would keep the two younger recruits that had some 'vim' about them, and who reminded him a bit of himself in his younger days. Instead, he would continue Hamish's move into telephone sales, and embrace the world of social media.

The business also used a number of commission agents or freelance sales-people, mostly from the various agencies that provided such services. While they were undoubtedly cheap, as they were only paid on completion of a successful sale and could be flexed with demand, he also knew that they usually sub-optimised on opportunities by not up-selling enough. He had therefore called Sales Manager Ian Long into his office to voice his concerns.

"Hi, Ian, just wanted to chew over a couple of things with you about our approach to sales. We both know the danger of freelancers, so I wanted to check out the situation, particularly with respect to reputational damage."

"Not sure anything's come my way in that regard, Toby. You know those sorts of things are handled by Edith."

"Yes, sure. But I'd like you to take a look personally. You're much closer to the action, and can talk directly to the sales team to see what they might have picked up. They've been around a bit now, so they should have a few listening posts established for their own purposes?"

"I'll have a go, but can't promise anything. They are all very busy trying to reach their targets," replied Ian. "But a review of our approach to sales would be a good thing."

Knowing the importance of having good data for the successful running of a business, Toby had pressed on, "Of course - and this is strategically important, so we must make time for it. I was hoping you could do an audit of performance to see what returns we *are* getting from freelancers, and whether you could track down any customer complaints that had originated with any of them? And while you're at it, we again both know that resellers are more reliable, and can gain us access to markets our door-to-door sales approach can't reach, so could you look into increasing the number of resellers we use? A short report will be fine."

"No promises," replied Ian. "I'll see what I can fit in."

After briefing Ian to increase the number of resellers and cut out the poor-performing freelancers, he turned his attention to their current lead generation activities. This was clearly a key issue, and with social media dominating the communications channels, the need for a strong presence was reinforced. Currently, communications were the responsibility of Gilbert Turkey, and seemed to revolve around adverts in local press, fliers distributed in various likely suburbs, and some direct mail activities. There appeared to be no real pattern or structure to these, leaving Toby with an impression that it was all a bit arbitrary. He decided to bite the bullet and talk to Gilbert about the issue, to see what might be done to improve things.

In his meeting request, Toby had asked Gilbert to come along with his communications plan. On arrival, Gilbert had been a bit aggressive, and wanted to know why Toby was trying to interfere with his area. After a while, it became clear that there was no plan, and that decisions to advertise were based on that month's special offers that he was contacted about. Leaflets etc. were based on Gilbert's instinct (he claimed to have a very good nose for opportunities), or reports from sales people that there were good opportunities in this or that area. His 'watchword', he said, was 'value for money'.

"Okay," Toby had responded. "I like value for money. Tell me about your budget. I've not seen anything in the company financial information to indicate what that looks like."

"Oh, we don't work with such bureaucratic devices here," Gilbert had replied. "That's very much 'big corporate', and as you know, we are a smaller, family business. We rely on good relationships rather than inflexible targets and expenditures. We have to move with the market as it changes and fluctuates. Take opportunities as they arise. That takes nous and judgement to get the right level of enquiries."

"In my experience, and I've worked in a fair number of SMEs," Toby explained, "budgets are very common and important for the management of the business. I think we ought to be establishing a budgeting process to know what's happening."

"I think if you have any worries about the financial side of my area, you should talk to Paul Travers. He signs off all my expenses and has never raised any concerns. It sounds to me like a lot of extra work, which will undoubtedly interfere with my, and probably others', ability to do our work. If you want my advice, I don't think you're going to get very far by marching in here and disrupting well-established ways of working."

"No, no; my desire is only to take the business forward on a profitable growth trajectory," Toby had responded. "I don't want to hamstring anybody. In fact, the opposite. We just need to make sure things don't get out of control."

"Difficult word 'control'. Goes with 'command', you know, command and control? In my experience, that often leads to cuts. Cost-cutting to improve the bottom line, just like Hamish. Mark my words, that's not a good way forward. I'm afraid it didn't do him any good, even though I really like him as a father-in-law."

The last line was said with some degree of emphasis. Toby had taken this to mean that Gilbert was reminding him of the family ties that Toby himself did not have. Toby had felt he needed to move on,

"Well, a different issue would be the Return On Investment (ROI) you're getting from the different streams of marketing activity?"

"I thought that was pretty much a dead duck. No-one really knows what they're getting. I'm sure you know the famous quote: *'I am convinced that about one-half the money I spend on advertising is wasted, but I have never been able to decide which half*?"

Feeling that he was in danger of a confrontation he did not want to have, Toby had then ended the conversation, "Okay, well I think there *are* methods around these days, and it would be good if I could ask you to look into the area? It would be great for all of us to understand the territory. Perhaps a plan for the next 12 months and some analysis of the return on investment would be very helpful for the team."

He had received a cursory nod in response, and Gilbert had left the office, clearly irritated. Toby had then made a mental note to follow up with Paul Travers to see what sort of expenditure Gilbert was operating with. It was only after Gilbert had left his office, that he wondered if he should have given him more of a steer on where to start investigating marketing ROI, and some deadlines for review of progress and delivery.

The Move into Social Media

Given the unsatisfactory responses he had received from Gilbert, Toby decided that he definitely had to make the move into social media if they were going to increase the number of leads they generated. After some consideration, and as it was a world in which he was not entirely experienced, he commissioned a reputable website design company to update the Eternal website with SEO features, and a marketing agency to orchestrate a blog and devise a social media strategy.

Theoretically, these should have been the responsibility of Gilbert. However, it seemed that Hamish had never officially passed on the responsibility for the website, so Toby was able to simply pick up where Hamish had left things. Indeed, feeling that he was probably the only person equipped to manage this sensibly, it made sense for Toby to take personal charge of overseeing this work. It had seemed the only workable way forward.

Like most similar projects, costs had overrun, but having already invested £20K, it was clearly too important a move to abandon. Later, he managed to squeeze another £10K for the project in spite of initial resistance from both the chairman and Paul Travers. At that point, he had also asked to recruit one of the consultants to manage the digital side of the business. With hindsight, he could see how this must have looked to the board, i.e. more expense, and perhaps a little bit of 'empire building'. But at the time he was enthused by the idea of much greater sales leads that would cover the costs, which the marketing agency assured him were imminent. Had he perhaps been too carried away with the excitement of a potentially significant initiative, and maybe placed too much faith in the marketing agency?

Given the problems of working with Gilbert, Toby had decided that he needed to do most of the content creation and themes for the blogs etc. himself as well. This had led him face-to-face with the knotty issue of competitive positioning. Apart from one very large dominant supplier, most solar companies were of a similar size and ilk to Eternal Energies. Some majored in innovation, and others in technical expertise, with many positioning themselves on price and 'being local'.

Having been one of the first in the market, Toby decided that the best position was to present themselves as the most experienced; a safe pair of hands in a fast-developing industry. This was at odds with Gilbert's focus on using attractive prices as the 'door-opener', and leaving it up to Ian Long and the individual sales person to pursue the sale according to their preferred approach. Toby had the impression that this often came down to price, but he had no evidence to back this up. Toby's view was that they were not in a position to compete on price, as there were no real economies of scale open to them, and he believed that positioning them as 'the original solar panel company' would put them in a more powerful position. In addition, he recognised that having a 'green tinge' would probably be helpful given the fairly widespread commitments to Net Zero, and increasing concerns about global warming and the environment. He still believed that this had been the right approach.

As time progressed, Toby had had to devote more and more of his time to the social media platforms that had been developed for the company. Gilbert had become distinctly sulky, and none of the sales-people showed any inclination or indeed, competence, in the area. Most of them relied on being good at 'working with the customer' once they had a good lead. They were not the most dynamic or creative people, but they had managed to do enough 'deals' to keep turnover growing under Hamish. The average installation value was between £12 and £30K, so ten to twelve sales per sales-person a year worked well for the business.

The Path to Growth

Apart from his work on digital communications and the Monday SMT updates, plus the regular foray into the office and workshop for a bit of 'Management by Wandering Around' (MBWA), Toby had spent the following 6 weeks locked in his office working on social media, and getting to grips with the market opportunities he had identified prior to joining the business. Such analysis had been one of his major strengths in his previous positions. There were currently seven different types of solar panel on the market, of which Eternal Energies now supplied five. This included the original thermal and photovoltaic panels on which the company had been founded, plus a range of other energy-generating panels.

Missing from their range were transparent and thin film panels. At the same time, there were some innovative generating panels in development in various parts of the world. In other words, this was an industry in a state of fairly rapid technological evolution, which would surely lead to market opportunities opening up, particularly if the government and corporations began working on the tricky path towards 'Net Zero'. Toby made a mental note to keep abreast of developments, and to put in place a system for monitoring innovations, perhaps using a press cutting agency. As he sat in the pub, Toby reflected that this had also remained in the 'not urgent' box. Too much to do when you have incompetent staff, he thought angrily to himself.

Transparent panels were ones that could be fixed to glass, and which would allow some light through while generating electricity. Their low efficiency made them unsuitable for domestic application, but if applied to industrial and commercial buildings, where there were many hundreds (sometimes thousands) of windows, generational savings could be significant.

Thin film panels were similarly relatively inefficient compared to other panels, but their main asset was their flexibility. This meant they could be fitted in small and awkward spaces, wrapped round pillars and chimneys, and used on mobile homes etc. At that time, however, they were not widely available, and so could be very variable in price and lead time for supply. Toby had also reasoned that this was more a niche market and probably not for Eternal.

After a while, it became clear to Toby that if they were going to get any significant growth, they would have to diversify into non-residential markets. While the market for household installations was growing (albeit slowly), and sales were holding up, there had been significant volatility in demand. This reflected the availability of government subsidies, the state of the economy, environmental awareness, and energy prices in general. In addition, break-even on the cost of installation was roughly 8-13 years, so few domestic users were investing for economic reasons. Similarly, housebuilders had demonstrated a reluctance to add expensive additions to new builds that were only going to achieve payback for the purchaser in the longer term, and who might already be at the limit of their finances. Only government initiatives would change that, and they tended to be unpredictable.

The obvious segment to go at, with the greatest range of opportunities, was industrial and commercial buildings. IKEA had already installed solar arrays in a number of its properties, and Toby felt sure there would be many interested in following suit. For this, they would need to add transparent panels to their range, and find building surveyors familiar with this segment that could assess the potential for any installation, and specify requirements. Currently, Eternal Energies employed one part-time surveyor for their direct sales to residential customers, but who seemed to spend most of his time travelling. He was most certainly completely unqualified to look at industrial or commercial premises, and had no knowledge of transparent panels. Toby would also need some sales-people that could work in Business-to-Business (B2B) markets, as the sales process would be very different from selling to a residential home owner.

Toby remembered being enthused by the analysis as he began to look at some rough estimates of the numbers. The transparent panels worked out at between 50-75% cheaper per square metre than most other forms of panel, and had a longer expected life, so there were definite benefits to be emphasised in any sales pitch. The rest would be about cost savings on power consumption from the grid, plus the income potential from selling surplus electricity back to the grid. This would be in addition to their Corporate Social Responsibility (CSR) credentials. Installation would potentially double the cost per panel, but leave an operating margin of about 45%. His next step was the preparation of a plan.

The Senior Management Team (SMT)

By the end of his first three months, Toby realised that he had been trapped in his office for far too long and needed to get more involved in the business. Besides, he recalled, he was approaching the end of his first 100 days, and needed to ensure that favourable first impressions were well embedded. He remembered reflecting that he hoped people would have been impressed by the hard work he had put in on creating a social media presence, and the new positioning he had developed. He also hoped that people would be aware of his desire to keep a lid on costs, having sent round an email on budgets following his conversation with Gilbert. He also felt sure that people would be pleased with the improvements Bob Meadows would undoubtedly have been implementing. He had left Bob very much to his own devices, having briefed him on his arrival to 'shake up' operations, and 'lick customer service into shape'.

"So, what do you think is wrong with the way things are at the moment?" Bob had asked.

"They are just clearly inefficient. It seems to take a long time between the sales people delivering an order, and that order being fulfilled. On virtually my first day, I had an email from a customer complaining that she had agreed to an installation six weeks ago, paid a holding deposit, and had heard nothing since in spite of having made a complaint. She had got my name from an internet search, and hoped I would at least be able to give her an indication of when something might happen. I passed it to Edith and Gilbert, but each thought the other had sorted it – although I'm not sure Edith had intended to do anything. I'm sure with your experience, you will be able to get to grips with that sort of thing."

"Well, you never know. There could be any number of issues at play there. I'll certainly have a good look at that."

"And that's another thing," Toby had gone on. "I'm not at all sure that Edith is right for customer service. It would be much better if you could wrest control from her, or at least get her reporting to you. She doesn't seem that comfortable, so I'm sure she would be glad for someone else to take over. See what you can do."

The Away Day

Following that conversation, and to make up for the lack of management meetings since the first after his arrival, Toby had decided that an 'Away Day' was in order. He sent round an email to each of the SMT, asking them to prepare a presentation for the meeting. In this, he had asked for strengths and weaknesses, highs and lows, performance against budget, and plans for the next three months. Underpinning these requests was his belief that to run a business successfully, the CEO needs to know what's going on, and what the numbers look like. Otherwise, decisions would be based on inaccurate assessments of the state of the business, or even personal preferences. The lack of solid information about the business had frustrated him then, and still did to this day.

Annabel had booked them a room in a nearby pub, and they had gathered there for coffee and pastries at 9.00am. Toby had issued a running order for the presentations, and had allocated an hour for each team member. He had opened the show by reiterating his desire for people to be open and honest with each other, and to look for the positives that could be built on over the next three months. He had also put himself down last, so that the final hour could be devoted to small group discussions about how best to implement his growth plan.

Unfortunately, no-one had been able to compare performance against budget as there *were* no budgets. Wondering why he hadn't spotted that before, especially given his meeting with Gilbert, he made a note to address the issue with Paul Travers; along with the other issues he had spotted, such as the information for the auditors. Few managers were able to identify any weaknesses, and plans for the next three months were patchy. Only Bob was more open, and had laid out improvements he was looking for in other areas, and announced that he felt customer service definitely did need to be transferred from Edith Smalley to his area. Toby had noted that heads had dropped when Bob mentioned this. The reason, he reflected, was probably that they knew Edith was going to react badly to the idea. He was aware that Bob had already raised the issue with her, and Toby had hoped any issues would be resolved by now. As it turned out, she had not been relieved to shed the responsibility, and had probably complained to the board and other members of the family. In retrospect, he saw that he might have been a bit too hasty with his assumptions about her motivations.

"I don't know about the rest of you," Edith had said between gritted teeth, "but I did feel very intimidated by Mr Meadows when he talked to me about giving up customer service. First Mr Thunder, and then Mr Meadows, have basically criticised me for doing my job. Hamish had been very clear about what to do, in particular, with complaints, and now I'm being told that we've got it all wrong. It doesn't feel right. It's a basic principle that if most customer complaints are let lie, they usually disappear. Only those that were still being pursued after three or four months should be acknowledged and addressed. It's a question of disruption and the impact on costs. I'm getting very stressed about this, and would appreciate a bit of respite."

She had not become hysterical during the meeting, but it was obvious that she was very upset and felt the pressure of a lingering loyalty to Hamish. This, plus Bob's proposal for her to now report to him, was clearly a bit too much for her. At the time, he could see that this was going to be a difficult one to resolve, particularly with the chairman's view that she was a 'family favourite'.

Toby had planned for the presentations to last till well after lunch. In fact, they had fizzled out by 12.30pm. After a buffet lunch that featured most people on their phones rather than talking about the morning's discussions, he moved to his own presentation on social media developments, and the first 'great reveal' of his plans for growth with appropriate targets.

The response from the small groups on implementation, however, had not been encouraging, and the feedback had been more about why his proposals couldn't be implemented, than how they could.

"Okay everyone," he had said in closing the meeting. "My job here is to set direction, and it is clear that this is the direction of travel we need to take. I think what we all need to do now is to look at our areas, and think about how we can embrace these new opportunities. Perhaps we can all develop an implementation plan for presentation at the next meeting? Let's say, in two months' time. Good work today, and thanks, everyone, for your hard work," he had finished, even though he thought they had been particularly weak.

Looking back, Toby reflected that one of his key strengths had always been his ability to analyse opportunities, even though it often took him some time to arrive at a clear focus. Essentially he was a 'data nerd', and always wanted to make sure he had covered all the angles, which meant that he was thorough, if a little slow. He realised that this went with his rather introverted nature. The outcomes, however, had stood him in good stead in his previous roles, and had probably been one of the factors that had got him the job at Eternal. He had therefore found it surprising that the SMT had not been more engaged with his analysis and conclusions, and still wondered how he might have engaged them more. To be a leader, one needs followers, Toby reflected, but had never got the impression that the people at Eternal had aligned themselves with his direction of travel. One to think about, he said to himself.

5

TROUBLE WITH FINANCE

As Toby gazed at the swans, two began having contretemps. This took him right back to Paul Travers. Indeed, Toby physically shuddered when he remembered his first encounter with the company finance manager. Perhaps as an early warning sign that the job of CEO was not going to be quite as easy as he had imagined, Paul Travers had given him the shivers from the word go. His father had been finance manager before him, and had helped Angus Smalley start the business. Being a cautious man, he'd never invested in the business himself, so Paul was part of the furniture but with no equity interest.

In spite of this he was a director of the business, attended board meetings, and helped the NED with some of the family trusts. During his first week, Toby had invited all senior staff to make an appointment to come for coffee and a chat. Paul had been the last to answer, and it wasn't until three weeks later that Toby realised that he still hadn't seen Paul. When he finally came to see him, Paul had been late. At the first meeting he had been politeness personified, if a little monosyllabic. It wasn't until later Toby recognised that underneath the polite exterior, he had undermined him on a number of issues. At that meeting, Paul had intimated that Toby knew little about the way the business ran, and their particular product range, but in a way that sounded sympathetic.

"I know you have been very busy since arriving, and probably haven't had time to understand the business and technical issues involved with our products yet. Although we are small, it's quite a complex business. It usually takes new people some time to get up to speed. There are so many factors to take into consideration. Not at all easy." And later, "Well, sadly I'm just an accountant and don't have the benefit of an MBA. Wish I had, just never had the time or the opportunity."

From then on Paul made minimal contributions, except to question the wisdom of some expenditures, and the high salary that had been offered to Toby's recruit. The cause had been revealed when he had arrived for his meeting following the Away Day. First, he was again late arriving at Toby's office, and then had brushed aside the offer of a coffee. When Toby began to ask Paul about the scope of his job, he again received monosyllabic answers. Eventually, Toby had asked him whether he had a problem. At that point, the torrent was unleashed.

"Everyone thinks the board made a mistake appointing you," he had said. "There are well-qualified people in the business and frankly, no-one's been impressed by you so far, particularly as they haven't seen that much of you. And then there's the car and the Apple laptop - when we all use Dell and Microsoft - the iPhone, and the designated car-parking spot. I mean, why are you so special that you are the only one in the business with a designated parking spot? The rest of us all have to fend for ourselves? How does that help you run the company?"

For Pete's sake, Toby had thought to himself; what impression did Paul think he and his shabby, rather musty office, gave customers? Paul was short, slightly overweight, and with very poor dress sense. Any highstreet retailer could provide an off-the-peg suit that would look better than the one he was wearing, and would definitely look a bit less shabby. Apart from being rude to Toby, it seemed that Paul was also rude to customers and suppliers. Indeed, one of the younger salespeople had later confided in him that Paul had actually accused a customer of climbing onto the roof of his house to deliberately sabotage the array they had recently installed, so that he could get a reduction in the bill.

Sometime later, Toby came to see that Paul was actually so full of resentment because he felt that he had personally been responsible for much of the success of the business, but that family members had never recognised his contribution or paid him his full worth. He had been surprised that he had not even been interviewed for Toby's job. So here was a big problem: what to do about Paul Travers? The chairman had appeared unsympathetic when Toby had later raised the issue at one of their infrequent one-to-one meetings.

"You know, Hamish didn't have any problems getting Paul to do what was needed," the chairman had responded. "But you're the CEO now, and as you have expressed several times, you simply need to show leadership and make it clear what's required. I recognise that Paul can be a bit awkward, but he seems to know the business inside-out and should be a valuable source of knowledge. We, the board, had seen him as potentially being your right-hand man. And if you feel that Paul needs to modernise the accounting procedures or anything else, perhaps you could work with him on the changes required? After all, you have held senior roles before."

Not wishing to show his unfamiliarity with accounting, Toby had agreed to give it a go, and to consider what else might be needed; although he was already clear about what some of them might be!

Two weeks went by, and Toby was at his wits' end. Paul still wasn't co-operating and was showing no inclination to work with Toby on a system upgrade, let alone produce the information Toby had repeatedly requested.

"No time," Paul had explained. "The main problem is the auditors. They're being particularly difficult, inflexible and overly demanding. We had the same problem with the last lot, but thought that these would be different. They have been very threatening recently, and have implied that they may refuse to sign the accounts. I'm sure we'll resolve it; I always have! They have clearly forgotten who the customer is!"

After a further meeting with the chairman, it was agreed that if Toby couldn't work with Paul, he could make him redundant. Although the business didn't really need a finance director, the best way was to replace Paul with someone of that calibre, as Paul wasn't sufficiently qualified. In a closed session without Paul, the board had reluctantly agreed, and Toby made preparations to replace him with someone else he knew that had just come onto the market.

The termination interview had not gone well. Luckily, Toby had the company's external HR consultant in the room, but that hadn't stopped Paul accusing Toby of victimisation, discrimination, and unfair dismissal. He had followed these up with solicitor's letters claiming £2 million compensation, supported by doctor's notes for stress and work-induced depression, plus other health problems from working in a poorly-ventilated and damp office.

It took Toby five solid days' work to recall and document examples of Paul's insubordination, find supporting emails, build the case for a finance director, consult with the company lawyers, and the HR consultant, and then write up the whole case for redundancy. In the end, they had come to a compromise agreement, and the board had agreed on a suitable package in recognition of Paul's history with the business, and with what was felt to be the 'family discomfort' from Paul leaving. The package was nowhere near the amount claimed.

The replacement, Christina Casey, started one month after the settlement had been completed. In many ways she was a stereotypical accountant: introverted, quite awkward socially, but intellectually very capable. Once again, she was someone Toby had worked with, albeit some time ago, when she was still working towards qualification. Following a break to have children, she was now a fully qualified financial accountant, with a number of successful financial roles on her C.V, and ready for a more senior position. She recognised that this would probably mean moving to a smaller company. It was therefore fortuitous that Toby had contacted her when he had, with the offer of the role of finance director, with a board appointment at Eternal Energies.

Although there was an accounts department that shared the three office staff, not much work had been done during the process of managing Paul's exit. Toby had made it clear soon after he arrived that he expected people to work hard and to use their initiative, and he had emphasised this to the accounts staff when he'd broken the news of Paul's departure to them. Unfortunately, it seemed that Paul had kept a lot of information close to his chest, and the staff had no idea what to do.

'Oh well,' he had thought to himself, *'better to wait for Christina to arrive. I don't want to undermine her before she's even started. And they're an awkward bunch; quite loyal to Paul.'*

The removal of Paul Travers as finance manager had taken place six months from Toby's start date. Sitting by the river slowly drinking his Speckled Hen, Toby ruminated, rather mournfully, that he had been right about Paul from the word go. From the time he had avoided his early meetings, demonstrated considerable disrespect by being late, and his painfully polite sarcasm, to his complete disregard for the financial information he had been requested to produce, and his final outburst, he had both undermined Toby and sabotaged his ability to get on top of the numbers. Not only had this hampered his decision-making and ability to take the business forward, but it had also resulted in an inability to provide relevant data to the board, which had reflected badly on him.

Perhaps he should have acted earlier? But then there had been the chairman's initial support for Paul, and the feeling that he was seen as a valued member of the senior team by the family and the rest of the board. Should he have followed his gut and been stronger, or would he just have been creating a rod for his own back? It was hard to tell now that he had been fired, but the question still left him with conflicted feelings about what should have been the 'right' thing to do.

Worse for Toby was the fact that Christina turned out to be a great financial accountant, but poor people manager. She had forensically sorted out the trusts that Paul had run with the NED, and narrowly saved the company from a significant tax bill and fines from HMRC, resulting from a number of unaddressed legacy issues missed by both Paul and the NED. But when it came to implementing an updated accounting system, she couldn't seem to get the cooperation she'd needed.

In one conversation, she had said, "To be honest Toby, I am beginning to wonder whether they are intellectually up to the job. Maybe that's why Paul had kept so much of the work to himself. I can see myself going the same way. Or have they just not been sufficiently well trained?"

"Could be, Christina," Toby had replied. "But one of the advantages of having someone like you, is that I'm sure you'll be able to bring them round and get them trained for the job. I didn't employ you just for your good looks, you know, you are very well qualified as well." Actually, he reflected, he hadn't employed her for her looks at all.

"Look, Toby, if you think I've got time for remedial education, think again. I've already saved the business more than my salary in potential tax penalties and fines. And that has taken a great deal of hard work! And frankly, I'm getting a bit fed up with all the increased absenteeism, doctor's notes signing people off for stress, plus the odd bout of tears about how unfair I was being. Unfavourable comparisons with Paul aside, they just seem to get very resentful when I ask them for information, or to do a simple task. And by the way, I think commenting on people's appearance is unbecoming of a CEO."

As Toby watched the swans, he remembered having some sympathy with trying to work with uncooperative staff after all his experiences. However, what on earth was wrong with a few compliments?

The company finances had been reliant on spreadsheets, and an out-dated accounting system that was no longer supported by the original developers. With a brief to transfer the company's accounts onto a modern package, Christina had chosen one she had used in her previous appointment, even though it was probably far too sophisticated for Eternal Energies, with much unnecessary functionality. Being a qualified accountant, and having left her days as an accounts assistant far behind her, Christina struggled to transfer data herself. In addition, without the technical support from an IT department, and having been refused the use of consultants by the board, she had also found it difficult to get the various bits of the new system talking to each other, or to incorporate data from the old system. These were all tasks that she was used to getting other people to do. Furthermore, of course, the difficulty of increasingly unhelpful staff had only compounded the problem.

Eventually, she recognised that she had to recreate the accounts from the bottom up if she was going to get anywhere, and to relearn some of her old basic accounting skills. Accordingly, she had introduced new accounting codes for income and expenditure, along with new ways of structuring and entering data into the system. In the previous processes nothing really matched, and had, in any case, been a bit haphazard. It had then been the Devil's own job to get people to use the new system properly, and as a result reports remained unreliable, and variations and variances were hard to explain for some time. Toby's difficulty in presenting good information continued, in spite of Christina now being a board member.

Over the ensuing weeks, the support/accounting staff (payroll, invoicing/accounts receivable and bookkeeping) slowly left the business. In retrospect, Toby wished he'd got someone to do exit interviews with them so that he could have picked up the problems earlier. It wasn't till much later that he discovered that they had found Christina unclear in her requests for work, unsympathetic when faced with personal problems, and rather patronising when explaining things. The problem was that the business needed a financial controller rather than a person of Christina's attributes.

Had I been wrong to appoint an over-qualified person to the role? Or had she just proved too difficult to manage? Surely someone in a senior management role would have been better at handling staff than Christina? Or had I been wrong to assume that would be the case? But then I had also been restricted by the need to create a new role in order to make Paul redundant. Was there a different route I should have taken? No easy answers there.

6

MEETINGS, BLOODY MEETINGS

While Toby had been wrestling with the issue of Paul Travers and working towards his removal, the regular Monday SMT meetings/briefings had also been rather fraught events. Paul had obviously got wind that something was afoot, but the team remained as; Toby, Gilbert Turkey, Ian Long, Edith Smalley, and Paul Travers (who rarely attended anyway), with the new addition of Bob Meadows. Unfortunately, the amount of sniping at each other had not subsided. Not enough was being achieved, and Toby's time was spent calming people down and troubleshooting customer and supply problems, as well as managing the Social Media activities. He still could not fathom why they were so antagonistic towards each other. He usually managed to develop quite harmonious teams.

With the departure of Paul Travers and the introduction of Christina Casey, the atmosphere remained frosty. And after the outburst from Edith Smalley at the Away Day, neither he nor Bob Meadows had been able to prise customer service away from her. This in spite of the fact that she had little else to do with the slow departure of the support/accounting staff after Christina's arrival. So far no replacements had been appointed. At the same time, the board kept requesting more detail, as their frustration with the lack of any solid data had grown. Toby thought about how unfair this had been, given that it was not his fault that the board had refused resources to sort out the problems and, in any case, Paul Travers's data had very likely been wildly inaccurate. At least they would be on solid ground once Christina had rebuilt the accounting system, but that was some way off.

A further problem was that it seemed many staff were becoming disgruntled and demotivated. Whispers had reached him that staff were not sure what to prioritise or where they were going. What had the various SMT members been doing? Toby had wondered at the time, and still did. However, it wasn't until much later that he recognised he had not addressed one of the basics and created a 'Vision and Mission Statement'. He had learnt that all good organisations used these, although he'd never written one himself. He had resolved to address that at some point.

What seemed to be happening was that some staff were going behind Toby's back to complain to Gilbert, Edith, Hamish (when he was around) and the chairman about how the atmosphere had changed. Toby had hoped that Bob Meadows would have been able to keep people in-line and enthuse them, but it seemed that in spite of his people management skills, something more was needed. However, at the time, Toby was at a loss to work out what that might be.

He had hoped that the big meeting he had planned; the board meeting where he would present his growth plan, would set their minds at rest. Once approved, he had believed that a clear direction could be communicated to the rest of the business. Accordingly, he had spent a lot of time preparing his presentation. Come the day, he had first reminded them of his mandate on appointment: to grow the business profitably. He had then demonstrated how 'Business as Usual' was not going to do that in any spectacular way. Sure, the restructuring of the sales channels, plus the lead generation from social media were beginning to have an impact, but they would not double the business in the three-years'-time-horizon that they had indicated was required. Yes, solar panels would benefit from recently relaxed development regulations, but this support had not translated into the rapid growth experienced from 2010-2016. In fact, the majority of residential installations produced less than 4kW per hour i.e. were quite small, at an average of 10-15 panels depending on positioning and the make of panel. It remained to be seen how future government initiatives would boost residential demand. As ever, his analysis had been thorough and well thought through.

He had then taken them through the other possibilities, finally homing in on commercial/industrial buildings. His analysis demonstrated that this was the cheapest sector to go for, and presented a clear target of:

Small to medium sized, multi-site enterprises with buildings that had a good spread of window glass. They should have high energy costs, and a percentage of the buildings needed to have a 20-30 year expected life remaining.

He then went on to explain that this segment could be identified by market research, which would provide the newly dedicated salesperson with contact details, estimates of energy usage, and current energy supplier. This represented good value for money at £30K. Other market entry expenses would be the employment of a commercial building quantity surveyor (QS) training the installation team, insurance, a B-2-B salesperson to replace one of the lost residential salespeople, and stock-holding costs of transparent panels. Christina, who had joined the board in Paul's stead by then, was the first to question the strategy behind the proposal.

"Thanks, Toby. I think there are now a few more questions that it would be valuable for the board to explore. So, firstly, what exactly do you think social media is adding to residential sales?"

"Can't say exactly, Christina. You know how hard it is to link cause and effect with these sorts of things, but what we do know is that enquiries are looking more promising."

"Mmm. Well, looking more broadly, how would you quantify the size of the addressable market in the sector you've identified, given your definition of the target customer?"

"Haven't done precise figures yet," Toby had replied. "Didn't want to jump the gun, but very few commercial/industrial buildings have solar power, so we are looking at pretty large numbers. My guess is that in the average town in the West Midlands, there will be at least 50 opportunities, which, when multiplied up, will give several thousand in that region alone."

Christina had then gone on with further questions: How many installations did he envisage? What market share did that imply? Average sale value? Operating profit? Period of amortisation for entry costs?

Out of necessity, Toby remained a bit vague in spite of his previous analysis, but could see six installations a year adding £350-500K to turnover. This would hopefully grow over the period under consideration. Costs would be in the hands of Bob Meadows. Bob was invited to join the discussion in the board room, and made a good attempt at estimating likely costs based on six installations, and sounded on top of things.

Unfortunately, Christina's questions had created a note of caution amongst the rest of the board, who had eventually agreed to the proposal - but considerably watered down. There would be no market research, no surveyor, one of the existing sales team could be trained and then led by Toby, and the target would be six installations over the next twelve months. He wasn't quite sure how a target of six had been firmed up, but it seemed this was now set in stone.

Could he have managed that better, he wondered? Undoubtedly, but he had been hampered by the absence of good data, and being blind-sided by Christina's questions certainly hadn't helped. Maybe he should have talked to Christina in more detail beforehand, but he hadn't wanted to dull the impact of his strategy. *'Another question without a satisfactory answer,'* he reflected, as he stared at the swans slowly going about their business.

7

INTO THE UNKNOWN

Toby had been disappointed when he left the meeting, but at least had won approval to go for expansion into the new market, and could report positively to the SMT. He picked one of the two younger bright-sparks in the sales team, Albert, to be trained up. This was an area in which he knew he could do well. He then seriously addressed the possibility of Gilbert taking over the social media campaigns. Finding him at his desk, he invited him into his office.

"Gilbert, I have some good news that I'm sharing with you first before I let the rest of the team know. I have approval to get into the commercial/industrial markets, and so would like you to take responsibility for the social media projects. I've laid the foundations, so it's just a question of continuing in the same vein but with the extra dimension of the B2B markets. I'm sure you'll make a splendid job of it."

"Well, not sure about that," Gilbert had responded. "Having excluded me for the past few months, you now want to dump your workload on me. And you haven't exactly shared your thinking very widely. First you upset Edith by trying to take her job away from her, and now you want to load me up with extra work. Is there a pay rise or promotion that goes with it?"

"I'm afraid not, Gilbert, but you do get a chance to show your worth to the board. I understand that you were overlooked for my job, so now's the opportunity to impress and show yourself as a worthy successor?" Toby had hoped that the carrot of getting into the board's good books would be appealing, even though he suspected Gilbert didn't have a hope in Hades of becoming CEO.

"Okay, but I'll need a free hand. Unless you want to take me back through all the development work you did when you were locked in here in those early days?"

Toby knew full well that he had to hit the road almost immediately, and would not have the time or patience to laboriously take Gilbert through all the work he had done, plus handling the potential arguments that were likely to arise. Although he harboured misgivings about the havoc Gilbert might wreak on his campaigns, he felt he had no alternative if he was going to make a real success of this new, and very exciting, venture. He also knew that he was going to appoint Bob as his stand-in while he was out prospecting amongst commercial/industrial developments in the West Midlands and Kent motorways with the trainee salesperson, Albert, but hadn't wanted to reveal that to Gilbert, given how he had sold the transfer of social media responsibility to him.

Feeling relieved that he could devote his energies to more familiar territory, and trusting that Bob would make a good deputy in his absence, Toby felt invigorated by a new sense of direction and purpose. He took Albert with him on his travels and was reminded of himself at that stage in his career – full of energy and optimism. First, he had visited IKEA to see what they had done, and to pick up any tips he could. He then went on tours of commercial/industrial estates, mainly around Birmingham, Oxford and the Kent cross-channel warehouses. Cold calling was never easy, but Toby's earlier sales experience paid off, and he found that he was able to get appointments by literally knocking on doors and chatting up receptionists. He could see that the words *green energy* and *cost-savings* were an engaging proposition for many of the businesses they visited.

Particularly around the southern half of the West Midlands, pharma companies seemed to offer good prospects. However his lucky strike was finding a cold storage business with three sites, where the commercial director was an old customer from one of his previous jobs. He remembered Toby well, and thought his proposition very interesting. Acting as the introducer, he fixed appointments with the facilities manager, operations manager and finance director. They all seemed interested, and asked him to draw up a feasibility study with the help of their own part-time quantity surveyor (QS).

Eventually, they agreed to a pilot installation at their smallest site. All had gone well, although there was quite a lot of wastage as the installation team were not yet all that experienced. The major hiccup was getting permission to feed back to the grid from the relevant distribution network operator (DNO). Residential installations that required DNO registration had usually taken up to three months, and could be fast tracked. The much larger potential feed from this business seemed to require 12-24 months lead time, although cost savings from generating their own power began immediately. This meant a delay of sometime before the pilot could be fully evaluated. However, Albert had proved to be as bright as Toby had hoped, and had created a good visual case study that would be a valuable support for future sales pitches.

At the same time, enquiries for residential installations were indeed looking up from the push into social media, as he had stated to the board. Although in Toby's opinion, quality and quantity had suffered under Gilbert, qualified leads were being passed on to both the employed sales team, and third-party sales organisations. Closure remained difficult, but according to Ian Long, sales were improving. The key motivation seemed to be 'going green', which greatly pleased Toby, as this was an angle he had majored on in his digital communications. However, the figures were, as ever, vague, and even though positive, were still way below the increases required to achieve Toby's ambitious targets.

Toby remembered feeling very optimistic at that time, and thought he could see that his leadership was finally having an effect. He had taken the initiative to diversify into related markets even though it was a different product; he had faced down opposition, and risen to the challenge of the restrictions imposed by the board. In spite of the coolness between the senior staff, he felt that his interventions had prevented any major falling-out between them. Although he had yet to develop a mission statement, he also felt that the staff must at last have cottoned on to the company's direction of travel. In addition, he could see why the board had been reluctant to fully support the initiatives he had proposed: they were wary about the lack of hard performance data, and were protecting the profits available for distribution. 'Short-termism *in extremis*,' he thought to himself.

One initiative Toby had taken was to add a couple of social networking sites for professionals seeking contacts within an industry, but decided to manage these himself. To avoid Gilbert accusing him of undermining him once again, he had paid for these from his own pocket, to be able to create a target list of people and businesses for direct communications. He then, again out of his own pocket, enrolled a freelancer from People Per Hour, to develop and execute a communications plan for the networks supplemented by follow up emails. So far, he had received a number of warmish responses, and so had set about exploring entry points and qualifying their potential. Three stood out, and they had become his next focus accompanied by his up-and-coming sales trainee.

Eventually, one of the three had shown more than a passing interest and accepted a quote for a feasibility survey. Unlike the cold storage business, they did not have a QS, although they also had three sites. This required Toby to find a consulting QS on a freelance basis. He knew from previous experience that this would cost about £500 per diem plus expenses, and probably be at least a week's work. He wasn't sure if he could authorise a £3K engagement without going to Christina, since he had never officially been given any signing authority by Paul Travers, and the need had not arisen since Christina had arrived.

In the end, he phoned Annabel, "Hi, Annabel. Listen, sweetie, I need you to do me a favour if you would. I want to spend £3K on a freelance quantity surveyor for a really good sales opportunity, but have suddenly realised that Paul never gave me any signing authority. Could you sound Christina out and let her know what I need to do? If they confirm the project, we can build the cost into the materials' charge. The problem is that without a survey, we can't move forward, and the client seems unwilling to pay the upfront cost of one."

He hoped that an appeal from another woman might have more chance of getting permission than a phone call from himself, given the slightly frosty relationship that he had had with Christina recently. In the event, Annabel contacted Toby the next day.

"Morning, Toby, how's it going?"

"Surviving thanks, although these cheap hotels we're staying at have little to recommend about them. But I'm trying to keep costs to a minimum so as not to alarm the board; you know, keep them on side."

"Sounds fun – not! I've talked to Christina and she says it's fine to go ahead, although next time she'd like to have three quotes before agreeing. Meantime, she's authorised you to spend up to £2,000 on any one prospecting expense without the need to refer to her."

Whether it was Annabel's charm, the smallness of the sum, or the business case for the proposition, Toby never knew.

The new prospect was a biotechnology business with temperature-controlled labs and clean rooms, rather than cold storage facilities. However, they had a lot of glass and used a lot of energy. Again, they were restricted to the smallest unit; a laboratory on the outskirts of Banbury in the middle of a modern business park. The report from the QS demonstrated significant cost savings for the client, depending on the feed-in tariff to the grid they were able to negotiate. Battery storage for surplus energy required the construction of a separate out-building, but that didn't seem too expensive. The main problem area was the complexity of the building itself. The cabling required to support the equipment and information flows was significantly more involved than for the cold storage unit, and the need for good ventilation systems added to the intricacy of the building.

In spite of these, the business case looked solid, and the company decided to commission the work. However, problems began to arise when the scaffolders found that some of the surfaces they needed to fit the transparent panels to were very difficult to access, and the site health and safety regulations restricted the installation team's ability to work. Having learnt from their first installation of the potential for delay from the DNO, Toby had contacted them earlier, and they had promised a faster response.

Wastage also remained an issue because of the continued inexperience of the installation team, the difficulties of installation, plus the inaccessibility of some areas. This had led to a reduction in the output they could generate, throwing some of the cost-saving calculations out of kilter. And of course, the DNO proved unable to fulfil their promise. Toby's estimate was that the project should still produce an operating profit, but was unlikely to show a net profit. In addition, the delay in being able to feed-back to the Grid would delay the completion payment.

On the brighter side, Albert had shown great promise, and was eager to get going on his own. At the same time, Toby was very conscious that he had not been in the office for some weeks, apart from the odd flying visit, and remotely attending the Monday SMT meetings. Bob Meadows seemed to have been doing a reasonable job of keeping things going in his absence, but he was not the CEO. Toby had therefore resolved to let Albert loose to try his best on the road, and to return to Guildford to pick up some of the tasks that had lapsed in his absence.

In retrospect, this had been a good decision.

8

ANNUAL APPRAISALS

On his return, Toby discovered that Hamish had introduced annual appraisals as part of his efficiency drive and cost-saving efforts, six months before he left the business. In consequence, the arrangements for appraisals were a bit patchy. Indeed, the first Toby knew about the need for them was when the chairman had sent him a memo asking when he could expect to see the results, as they were now overdue. On quizzing Annabel, she had revealed that Hamish had indeed conducted appraisal interviews for the SMT, although he had not performed one with her. Back in the nick of time, Toby reflected!

"I could dig out the request email and Hamish's reports if that would be helpful," she had offered.

Toby was actually a bit jaundiced about the whole idea of appraisals, not having had a good experience himself. When he had conducted them for his sales teams, they had always followed a similar pattern, or 'dance' as he preferred to think of it. The person would fill out a questionnaire detailing their achievements over the year, areas they wanted to improve, long-term ambitions, and targets for next year. The last section was always the most important. The appraisee would enter a target, Toby would suggest a bigger target, and they would agree something in-between. Toby knew the appraisee would always underplay what they thought they could achieve, as their boss would always push for more. It was exactly what he had done when he was in their position, and what he would probably do himself when it came to be his turn to be appraised by the chairman and NED. *'All part of the game,'* he thought to himself.

The resulting report would be a list of achievements, some training recommendations that there was hardly ever enough budget for, a vague long-term objective (sales manager, working from home more etc), some sales targets, a bonus/pay rise recommendation (rarely forthcoming in full), and an overall performance rating. There were hardly any low scores, as most managers did not want to deal with disgruntled staff or to be too critical of people to their face. Looking through Hamish's reports, Toby could see a similar pattern emerging. No-one had scored below *Outstanding* with many achieving *Exceeded Expectations.* Everyone was, apparently, above average.

Recognising that this should have been started a month ago, he agreed with Annabel that she should send the SMT the email Hamish had used, but also remind them that they needed to conduct appraisals forthwith for their own staff. It was not until the email had been sent that he recognised only Bob Meadows and Ian Long actually had any staff reporting to them. All but one of Christina's had left, but they were due to leave soon, and Gilbert was on his own. Although Edith did have the receptionist officially reporting to her, she tended to operate independently. Apart from Christina and Toby, the others did have desks in the office, but were certainly not managed by Edith.

A week later, Toby began his appraisal interviews. He decided to bite the bullet and do Gilbert first.

Gilbert

He had wondered if he would be able to pin Gilbert down now that he had been *in situ* for some time, and whether he might have calmed down a bit. Sadly, he recalled, Gilbert had remained quietly hostile. He listed a considerable number of achievements, which Toby thought were actually just his day-job, couldn't identify any areas that he needed to improve, and felt that CEO should be his next role in the business.

"What about some of the targets we've discussed in the past?' he had asked Gilbert.

"Look, my responsibility is indirect sales, so I cannot be held accountable for sales themselves, as they are in the hands of others. And besides, Hamish had set my targets as 'to continue the good work in terms of emails, fliers and adverts,' as you'll probably see from his notes, if you've seen them. And I certainly have been doing exactly that in spite of the extra social media work."

Not much to get his teeth into there, Toby had felt. "Okay, what about the plan and analysis I had asked for when we had our talk just after I joined?" he had asked.

"Not sure I know what you're talking about," Gilbert had replied. "Can't recall any requests of that nature.

Besides, you had made it quite a difficult meeting. I do remember that. If you forward me a copy of the requests, I'll certainly take a look in my spam/junk box. Really don't remember seeing anything though."

Toby had cursed to himself that he had not done a follow-up email or recorded anything in his day book.

Gilbert had then gone on to say, "And while we're talking about responsibilities, can you tell me why you've set up a couple of professional network accounts without telling me? You gave me responsibility for social media, and then effectively cut me out of one part of it. It's the sort of thing people use as a case for constructive dismissal."

Not wishing to exacerbate the situation by telling him that he was useless, Toby had mumbled, "Look, Gilbert, it was a spur-of-the-moment decision and we were on the road, so not really an opportunity to keep you up to speed with everything. Been very busy. Besides, you've clearly been fully occupied with all the other social media activities. As you said, a lot of extra work." Toby had hoped that throwing his own words back at him would shut him up.

"That is true. But technically, it should come under my area," Gilbert had responded.

Not wishing to let Gilbert have the last word, Toby had closed with, "I know, but in this case, I think this is better managed by someone that is 'experiencing the hot breath of potential customers', as they would have an ear to the ground for the sorts of issues that needed to be aired. Anyway, that's my decision."

Putting the 'development of a communications plan', and 'producing some impact analysis' down as targets, Toby had reluctantly scored Gilbert as *Outstanding,* as he had no wish to live with the consequences of a low score. Gilbert, he reminded himself, had the ear of the family, and did not hold back when he felt aggrieved. He remembered not feeling good about himself for this act, but eventually brushed it off as expedient; all part of the politics of a family business, not that he endorsed 'playing politics'. In fact, he was at pains to avoid politics like the plague, and frowned on those he felt indulged in political manoeuvres. Anyway, Hamish had scored Gilbert similarly, so there was precedent.

Ian

Moving into more familiar territory, he next saw Ian Long, Sales Manager. Sales had been his bread and butter for many years now, so he was looking forward to a more comfortable interview. Ian had listed the installations achieved in the previous twelve months, and in the absence of a budget or targets, he was able to claim an excellent performance. Hamish's notes had indicated his desire for Ian to grow the business, and that he hoped he would be able to increase the average number of installations per salesperson, but did not include specific value or volume objectives. Toby decided that the best way forward was to think about what each salesperson might be expected to deliver, and how much greater that would be than for the various third-party vendors. He calculated that improving significantly on the previous year's turnover would only need one extra installation per salesperson at the average contract value to add £500,000 to the top line, and be in line with the ambitions set by the board. That plus the commercial/industrial additions should make a significant contribution to his targets. He was yet to figure out how the rest could be achieved with the limited resources at his disposal.

Ian had initially seemed to accept this, but had wondered what Toby felt were the priority areas. By this, he was referring to geographical focus, house type, and buying motivation. He also felt that the referrals from Gilbert didn't follow any pattern, and there had been a few blind alleys where salespeople had ended up wasting their time. In addition, there had been complaints from a few of the third-party vendors that the quality of the leads they were receiving was not very high, even though sales had improved. With regard to the increased productivity Toby was looking for, Ian also wondered how Toby would like to incentivise the team to go that extra mile.

"I remember clearly your introductory speech in which you promised an honest day's pay for an honest day's work, and that the extra mile would always be rewarded. The problem is that there hasn't been a commission or basic pay increase in the past two years, so I think you'll need to find something to sweeten the pill of higher targets. Besides, with your no replacement policy, we are one salesperson light, and we've lost that youngster to your commercial/industrial venture."

This had rather caught Toby on the hop. He had not been prepared for a pay negotiation, but not wishing to look stupid, he had agreed that he would raise the issue with the board.

"Good point," he had bluffed. "I had been wondering how pay had progressed before my arrival. No-one has really gone into that sort of thing with me, and it's been difficult to get a clear picture from any of the financial reporting."

"If you really want to know, I think an above inflation rise should be in order," Ian had retorted. "The last raise didn't compensate for the below inflation pay rises stretching back further. And if you're asking people to keep going at the rate that maintains current sales levels, let alone increase them when their take-home pay has reduced in real terms, you might find efforts drop off."

'Worse than negotiating with the unions,' Toby had thought to himself. *'Hadn't clocked Ian as part of the liberal left. Surely, he must see the need to constrain costs if there is to be any 'fat' to reward enterprise and innovation?'*

Promising once again to see what he could do, Toby had moved on to a second project that he had conceived while on the road hunting for commercial/industrial opportunities, "Speaking of effort and reward," he had continued, "with the new initiative to move into different markets, I was wondering if you felt any of the residential salespeople might be showing an interest in expanding their horizons now that we've had a couple of successes? The projects are bigger and therefore more profitable for them, and could well compensate for a lack of pay rises."

"No-one's jumping up and down, but I can certainly raise it again," Ian had responded, "but to be honest, I'm not really sure how to brief them. I know you've said commercial/industrial, but the list you produced was quite broad: warehouses, office blocks, factory units, laboratories, churches, schools, hotels, and conference centres. And there were others I can't recall just now. I think I need to give them a bit more direction so they don't waste too much of their time."

This had irritated Toby as he had been quite specific about the shape of the ideal customer:

> S*mall to medium sized, multi-site enterprises with buildings that had a good spread of window glass. They should have high energy costs, and a percentage of the buildings needed to have a 20-30 year expected life remaining.*

'How much more direction did they want?' he had fumed to himself. He had then reiterated the customer specification to Ian, and asked him to see what he could do about getting some of the salespeople more involved in the new markets. The young trainee he had extracted had certainly not found the transition too hard, so maybe this would encourage some of the others to explore the opportunities on their patch.

Toby had then ended the interview without really establishing Ian's longer-term objectives or areas for improvement. Still, the targets were clear, if not the priorities within them. And once again, Gilbert had reared his ugly head as a problem that was clearly interfering with the ability of the business to forge ahead in the market.

Toby remembered his concern about giving Gilbert responsibility for the commercial/industrial markets. *'Perhaps I should have created a separate website for business customers?'* he mused, *'And surely my emphasis on green issues in the earlier social media work I did would have given Ian a steer as to the priorities?'* Was it him, or was Ian just a bit narrow in his outlook?

Like Gilbert, Hamish had rated Ian *Outstanding* last year, and Toby felt he had to follow suit again. Given the rather bolshy behaviour he had just experienced, he didn't want to downgrade him to *Met Expectations,* given that he was relying on him to drive the improved sales performance he was looking for. He did feel a little apprehensive about the willingness of the board to countenance a pay increase for the sales team, given the priority they attached to dividends, but then he could always fall back on their reticence as an excuse when he went back to Ian.

Christina

The conversation with Christina had not been much easier. Having been with the business for a relatively short time, and given the need to overhaul the accounting system, Toby was able to agree some clear objectives with regards to the production of accounting information, and the setting of budgetary targets for the various parts of the business. However, the first sticking point arose when they talked about the departed staff,

"I can see the need for the targets, but there is a problem here, Toby. I do need to have some assistance. The one remaining person should be handing in her notice at any moment. I won't need another three people; one competent person would do. However, there are no good accounting technician candidates coming forward from Edith's efforts to recruit. I can manage a lot of the work by myself I'm sure, but it's not really my role, nor the role you promised me."

"I think the finance team was in a lot worse shape than I had thought," Toby felt forced to admit. "And I absolutely agree that you should *not* be doing the work of an accounting technician given your qualifications. Perhaps you could take another look at the applications you've had and see if there might be a hidden gem in there? Also, it might be good to see what you can get out of the remaining staff member?"

"Not much hope," she had replied. "I'm afraid she is clearly incompetent, uncooperative, and surly with it. And I'm certainly not going to nanny her."

Toby remembered wondering at the time how much of that was Christina's problem, and how much the assessment reflected reality. For sure they had all been graded very poorly on the appraisals that Christina had conducted almost immediately on arrival, pre-empting Toby's late move. He also wondered how much that had contributed to the sudden increase in absenteeism and sick leave.

'Not to worry,' he had thought. *'Christina herself is clearly financially competent, and appears to be getting to grips with the finances on a number of fronts, especially the potential tax liability from Paul Travers's mismanagement of the Trusts that would significantly affect cash flow and profitability.'*

Then he moved to a potentially trickier area,"One thing," he had gone on, "there's been a number of occasions that you've had to leave meetings to take phone calls, that frankly, have not been business-related. Now, we all have personal issues outside work, and the occasional call is acceptable. But you seem to get more than most, and I think you might try and reduce the number of times that people call you? It doesn't set a good example for the rest of the staff."

"I'm sorry, Toby, but it is an unfortunate fact of life that schools always try the mother first if there is a problem, no matter what you've told them. And these days, the things that count as 'problems' have multiplied significantly. If I see a call from the school, I have to take it in case it *is* something serious. You have two children yourself, so I would have thought you might have understood."

"Isn't there something you could do?" he had replied rather weakly.

"I don't know if you've ever tried to get schools to do something different for different people, but it always returns to the default person: the mother. Just a fact of life. And if you want to make an issue of it, you may find yourself on a hiding to nothing."

"Well, let's leave it for the moment," he had said, closing the conversation with some relief.

The issue of the difficulties with the replacement accounting system had not appeared by that point. Given the lack of history, he felt he also had to rate Christina *Outstanding,* as he didn't want to discourage her at this early stage in the development of the accounting function.

Next, he thought he'd better tackle Edith. He wasn't looking forward to that one either, so thought he would leave it to the next day, but it did have to be done.

Edith

As he entered the building the following morning with a cheery, "Morning, looking good today. Keep up the good work," to the receptionist, he began to appreciate why Hamish's 'bit of a sharpener' might have been useful. Wisely, he'd managed to resist the temptation since banning Annabel from offering one. Edith had begun by going through all her achievements for the year.

"Well, yes," she had started, "I've been very pleased with the complaints side of things and my responses to enquiries. Of the 20 complaints, I only had to pass three on to Mr Meadows… Bob. The rest I waited till they had followed up twice. The three I passed to… Bob had all made a third follow up, but I managed to delay them all for at least nine weeks. As Hamish used to say, only the serious ones persist. He would have been proud… as I hope you are too Mr Thunder… Toby. On the enquiries' side, four came to me for some reason. I tried to answer them, but had to pass them to Gilbert, as they had all related to either an advert he had placed or a flyer they had received. No idea what happened to them after that, even though I followed up with him. *'No need to worry,'* he'd replied, so I left it at that.

I've also been very busy with travel and accommodation requests, particularly from the sales staff, but also the chairman. Then there's the photocopying contract, the phones to keep on top of now that Mr Travers has left, plus the credit card receipts that I have to collect and collate for Mrs Casey… Christina. Obviously, with the reduced staff in the pool, I've had fewer people to look after, but ironically, that has meant more work for me, *and* the increase in absences has taken a huge amount of my time to sort out, plus advertising for a replacement. I had to think very carefully about the wording, given Christina's specification. I ended up with, *'Are you ATT Level One Award in Business Skills qualified? We have openings in our finance department for YOU!'* - the 'YOU' in capitals! I was quite pleased with that - *'Minimum wage guaranteed.'* We had a number of replies, but I'm not sure Christina was that impressed with any of them. Not sure what I could have done differently though."

Toby had inwardly sighed and decided not to pursue the obvious things that might have improved the quality of the responses. More important was trying to get customer service transferred to Bob. He knew from the

Away Day before he started that this might be a bit of an uphill struggle.

"Well," he had eventually replied, taking the opening of 'doing something differently' as an opportunity, "Now that you mention, 'what could be done differently', you know Bob has a great deal of experience in customer service?"

"Yes, he's mentioned it quite a few times. I've always thought that if someone has to keep repeating themselves about what they've achieved, they're probably over-egging it. Frankly, I'm not sure how much he *does* know about customer service. He's always mentioning that a fast response is important, but I know from Hamish that that is not the way to keep disruption to a minimum. Disruption is costly, he always used to say, and keeping on top of costs is a priority for us these days. I really don't understand where Mr Meadows… Bob… is coming from. Does he really not care about costs?"

"I'm sure he cares deeply about costs," Toby had replied. "As indeed do I! It's just that there's always a balance to be had and we need customers to be happy as well. You do know how important referrals are in our business as we have little recurring income? Referrals come from happy customers, and ones that feel ignored tend not to be happy." (*'Like talking to a five-year-old,'* he had thought to himself. *'Where do we go from here?')* "Look, I think that with your focus on costs, and Bob's focus on happy customers, you would make a great team, and really get that balance that I believe to be so important. What do you think?"

"I'm not sure how that would work, given his rather abrupt manner sometimes," she'd responded. "I'm sure he's lovely underneath; others have said that he can be very kind, but I must say, I do find him a bit of a cold fish."

Picking up the vague hint of a cue, Toby had soldiered on, "Well then, an ideal opportunity to get to know him better and see if we can get some of that famous synergy going that everyone talks about," he said, harking back to some of his MBA lectures, although he wasn't sure that Edith knew what synergy meant, judging from her expression. "Tell you what, let's put you and Bob together. As Bob is effectively my Number Two, it would be easiest if you reported to him anyway, especially now that I'm out of the office so often with this push into the commercial/industrial markets. That would make things much simpler for the both of us, and enable you to push forward with the expanded responsibilities you have these days. What do you say?"

"I'm not going to be forced into any substantial change like that. Give me some time to think about it and we can take it from there."

With that, Toby had closed the meeting and, like the others, had reluctantly awarded her an *Outstanding* on her appraisal report. Like Gilbert, she clearly had the ear of the family given that he could now see what the

NED had meant when he had confided in him on his interview day, and he didn't want any bad reviews coming from her in the other direction. Ruefully, he reflected as he sat in the pub garden, he couldn't remember following up with her either, and to this day, she still operated independently from Bob. Neither could he think of what had distracted him from following up such an important issue beyond just being too busy.

Bob was next on the list, but first he needed to fit in Annabel. He hoped both of these would be more productive and quicker than Edith.

Annabel

Annabel had run through her list of tasks and achievements. She was most pleased about the introduction of Toby to the business, and how she had enabled him to 'hit the ground running'. She was particularly pleased with the presentation packs she had prepared from his rather sketchy notes (she hadn't meant to criticise!) and her organisation of the SMT Away Day. In addition, she'd also done a bit of work for the chairman. It was not in her job description to do so, and although he did like to do most of his work himself, there were times when he had a bit too much on his plate. The rest had been about accuracy and getting things done on time.

"What about the future?" Toby had asked.

"Well," she had replied rather shyly, "I've been thinking about that. I've been here eight years now, and I think

I'm on top of the work. So, I was wondering whether there would be scope for me to do some HR training? People do seem to keep bringing me quite a few of their personal issues, and with all that business with Paul Travers, I thought it might be useful to have someone in-house, rather than that expensive external we use. Besides, I already help Edith with a lot of the workforce records, so I'm sort of in a HR role already."

"But surely Edith doesn't need help with those records; she should be able to do that herself rather than dumping on you?"

"She really seems quite busy these days, what with the staff leaving and all that. Keeping on top of all the comings and goings across the business seems to require more headspace than she has at the moment. Don't get me wrong, she's a lovely person, I just think she's a bit overwhelmed at the moment. It doesn't take a lot of my time. It's really good experience, and I do enjoy it. But it has made me think that maybe I could develop another side to my work."

Mindful that this was exactly the same route that his wife Sally had pursued, Toby felt he couldn't really object, even though it was HR. She had a good organisational brain and an attractive personality, so would probably do well in an operational role. However, he was not going to delve too far into the alternatives as it could get very complicated, so he asked instead that she look into the costs.

"As it happens, I have had a look," she had responded, "A foundation course would cost between £2.5 and

£3K, and I would be prepared to put some of my own money towards the fees. If the company could split it 50/50, I would just about be able to manage it."

Toby felt he had to agree, and asked her to prepare the forms. Inwardly, he groped around for the basis of the business case he would have to prepare to go with her application when requesting board approval. He'd always had trouble seeing the strategic value of HR, but he was sure he'd be able to come up with something.

The other point she had raised was about him. She had noted that he worked very hard and put in long hours, and was often the last to leave the building at night on the days that he was in the office. In spite of that, she felt that he sometimes sat on things a bit too long; some of the contracts she had put in his in-tray for signing for instance, and responses to memos from the chairman (who had eschewed the use of email or messaging and had retained a fondness for old-fashioned paper). She had explained that as she didn't really know what Toby spent his time doing, she wasn't in a position to help out.

"Sorry about that," he had explained, "It's just that I get an inordinate number of emails to sort through, and I don't want to miss anything important. Most are irrelevant, but there are some important ones that I have to deal with. Recently, for instance, there has been a lot of correspondence with the DNO companies about the new commercial clients' access to the grid for export, plus agreeing remuneration from their power supply companies for electricity they exported. And I'm never going to sign a contract without reading it first."

"Okay, I'm not sure what would be helpful for me to do, but what about acting as a filter and weeding out all the irrelevant correspondence? It could save you a lot of time."

At that point Toby had felt slightly embarrassed, as she would then see all the blogs he followed, the websites he had signed up for, and the odd game he used to help him relax. At least it was Pokémon and not porn! He was very anxious to maintain his image as a serious executive, and worried that if she could see some of the things that came into his in-box, a bit of his shine would be rubbed off. He decided to agree, but postponed a start until he had cleaned up the stream of inbound emails he regularly received.

Given Annabel's efficiency, there wasn't much he could suggest by way of targets outside the HR venture, except to carry on and not to let standards drop. He happily awarded her an *Outstanding* on her appraisal report, conscious that he needed to get these and the other reports finalised A.S.A.P, so as not to add to the impression of 'sitting on things'.

Bob

Bob had indeed been a very different kettle of fish. Unlike any of the others, he had started the interview by asking how Toby was, and how he was getting on with the push into new markets. Toby remembered feeling much more positive about the interview, and more confidently set about the appraisal.

Bob's achievements were certainly more solid than some of the, well, frankly puerile achievements of many of the others. He had found cheaper suppliers for a number of the products they carried, and he had reduced stock levels and got rid of some expensive redundant stock that had been cluttering the store room. Lord knows what they had been doing to the balance sheet. He had reached agreement with the complainants that had been passed his way, and persuaded them to post testimonials on Trusted Traders, and he had been working on some processes to try and improve the efficiency of order processing and installation. In addition, he had begun moves to get the company registered for ISO 9001.

'All good,' Toby had mused to himself at the time, "What about areas for improvement?" he had then asked, which is where things began to get sticky.

"One of the problems is that there isn't enough co-ordination between sales and operations. It's almost a classic case of two silos working separately with a high wall between us. Sales do their thing; get an order, but don't check with us as to its feasibility, be that in terms of configuration, quality or lead time. Sometimes they wildly underestimate the cost of installation, or promise installation in an impossibly short timeframe. We all know that it's the easiest thing in the world to sell a product if you customise the hell out of it, drop the price, and promise it tomorrow. Well, it often feels like that's what they're doing. The drive to increase sales, which I understand originated with your predecessor, looks to have become all-consuming. They seem to be battling to achieve their targets to the detriment of profit and delivering what the customer has been promised."

"Tricky one, that," Toby had responded, but not sure where to go next, "how do you think we solve it?"

"Well, I'm not sure it's 'we,' Toby," Bob had countered, "I think it's more *you.* I'm not in a position to take Ian on. I've mentioned it to him, but he simply says that his staff are overworked, underpaid, and are struggling to achieve the stretch targets imposed on them year after year. Neither of which is easy to challenge without a big row. You're in a much better position to see the bigger picture here, and to know what's really going on. He reports to you, so I think you need to sort out his priorities with him."

"I'll try and have a chat," Toby had answered.

"Another issue is the trade-off between cost, quality, and availability. As mentioned, I have found some cheaper suppliers, but they are not the same quality as some of the German products, or the better Chinese companies. And there can be issues with consistency of quality and availability. They come in containers and can often be delayed dock-side for a variety of reasons. Price also varies as both the price of raw materials and the cost of shipping is more of a lottery these days. From our discussions, I'm not sure what I should be emphasising; what are we most worried about?

Consistency? Cost? Quality? Or availability? How do these variables fit with the overall marketing and sales strategies, and how do they relate to our overall competitive positioning of being the 'original solar panel company'?"

"Good questions, Bob. I think we need to take time out to consider them, possibly at the next Strategy Away Day," Toby had responded.

"The other issue is customer service. I really can't agree with Edith's approach, and I think it's creating problems all over the place. People tell me that the move into social media has provided a platform, not just for us to promote ourselves, but also for a few bad eggs and disgruntled customers to let rip about us. Apparently, a couple of our competitors are also trolling us a bit as well. It's not a world I frequent, but I do know customer service, and I find it frustrating to have to deal with Edith, knowing how much better it could be."

"I know what you mean," Toby had agreed. "Well, I've put a proposition to her that would certainly improve matters. I now just have to wait and see how she responds. I can't go into it here, but I'll let you know the moment I get a response."

"Again, I think it's a problem only you can solve, Toby," Bob had continued, "It would be a great help to me, and I think to the business, if we could get resolution to some of these issues. You know the politics of the place better than me and are in a stronger position to deal with them."

"Not sure it's wise to play politics in my position, but I take your point. Trust me, I'm sure we can resolve most of these," responded Toby, not feeling quite as confident as he hoped he sounded. "The main issue of course is, as you say, family politics compounded by the muddled thinking of that pain in the posterior Gilbert Turkey, plus a sales force structure I inherited. Just haven't had time to address it yet. However, I'm sure you'll recognise that it is a bit of an uphill struggle. Hopefully a 'deep dive' at the Strategy Away Day will help sort things out."

Marking Bob as *Exceeded Expectations*, he hoped that the assessment would make him feel better about both his situation, and indeed, Toby himself. However, remembering Bob's parting shot as Toby was led out of the building on his last day, he suspected that it hadn't. Could he have done things differently? Another question to think about.

As he sat contemplating his time at Eternal, a swan had glided over to see if the pub clientele had left any scraps in the water. As there were none, the swan had headed back for the other side, looking disappointed. Sharing the sense of disappointment, Toby reflected on the appraisals and felt he'd missed a golden opportunity to stamp his authority on the business. To be sure, he'd been blindsided on his return to Guildford, having been completely in the dark about the need for appraisals, but he had a lingering feeling that he could have done better. Normally, he would have carefully prepared for each interview, collecting performance data to use as a basis for discussion. But in the absence of good data, and having been rushed into the process, he had been left at a disadvantage.

I knew that what I should have done was to let each appraisee know exactly where they stood in terms of relative performance, and to explore how they felt about their work, their team-mates, and the performance levels they had achieved. It's what I'd always done, and had helped keep my teams working well together. In this round, none of that had seemed possible. So, did the fault lie with the short notice, the absence of data, the belligerence of the people, the family connections, or had I simply not been brave enough? And if I had been brave enough, what would the consequences have been? Hard to tell, but rating a whole group above average had not, and did not, feel comfortable.

9

A BLINDING GLIMPSE OF THE OBVIOUS

Although Toby had inwardly agreed with most of the sentiments Bob had expressed during his appraisal, he had hoped that he had managed to suitably defend his position. He also recognised that Bob's words reflected another dilemma that was going to be difficult to address: the family dynamic, and its influence on the decisions that needed to be made. He felt as if he was in the middle of an Eternal Triangle, but not in the romantic sense. He smiled to himself as he enjoyed the play on words with the company's name.

Firstly; there was the family, who seemed to be focused on dividends and maintaining established staff and family relationships. Then there was the rest of the business, where there seemed to be a general reluctance to move forward at any speed, plus clearly some resentment and a cynicism about what was possible. And lastly, there was the market, which was diverse, difficult to pin down, and currently suffering from uncertainty about the degree of government support, in spite of all the espoused drive for 'net zero'. He could see that it was his job to reconcile these disparate forces, but it did feel like wading through treacle.

By this time, Toby's coffee and dessert had arrived from the pub kitchen. He was tempted to order a second whiskey, but remembered that he would have to phone Sally from the pub payphone to come and pick him up, and he didn't want to smell too much of alcohol. Hopefully, the coffee would disguise most of the fumes. Finishing his coffee, he settled back to stare once again at the swans on the river as they dived their heads into the water, in search of some tasty weed from the river bed. *'Fishing about in the weeds'* felt like another suitable metaphor for his year at Eternal, he reflected.

With a big sigh he returned to his contemplations, and remembered the shock he had felt when he had realised the potentially rookie-error he had made. The comments from Bob and Ian had resonated with everything he had learnt about business and corporate strategy on his MBA and elsewhere. What he had resolved and failed to do was create mission, vision and purpose statements as a starting point for his leadership of the business.

As he reflected, he couldn't understand why he hadn't seen the need for these when he had first joined the business, or even during his three months' gardening leave while he was waiting to start work. It was probably the distractions of moving, plus the omnipresent but subtle pressures from the three sides of the triangle; and in Gilbert's case, not so subtle. Still, it hadn't been too late, as there was a Strategy Away Day to be organised to address some of the questions raised during the appraisal interviews. His first dilemma had been where to start? Mission? Vision? Purpose?

Did the vision lead to the mission, or *vice versa*? And how were they different? He remembered his confusion at the time, and indeed, still found himself confused. In the end, he had decided to lock himself away in his office while he experimented with a couple of iterations to see if they clarified anything. His first shot was:

> *"Our mission is to be one of the leading suppliers of solar technology to both residential and commercial customers."*

But this had felt very much like a vision for where they wanted to be. It was not hard to replace the word 'mission' with 'vision.' Or, for that matter, the word 'purpose.' As he often did, he then turned to the internet to see if anything there would help. His first port of call was Wikipedia, where he found:

> *A mission statement is a short statement of why an organisation exists, what its overall goal is, the goal of its operations: what kind of product or service it provides, its primary customers or market, and its geographical region of operation.*

It had seemed to Toby that the only thing missing from his attempt was the geographical element. That was easily fixed, but actually didn't help differentiate a mission from a vision. When he had gone on to look at the examples from successful organisations commended as role models, to illustrate 'how it should be done', he again found it hard to understand how they differed from a vision. This was particularly true when he searched 'vision statements.' Once again, Wikipedia provided:

> *A vision statement is a high-level, inspirational statement of an idealistic emotional future of a company or group. The vision describes the basic human emotion that a founder intends to be experienced by the people the organization interacts with.*

One publication (Business News Daily) that targeted younger and smaller businesses carried the definition:

> *A vision statement is a written declaration clarifying your business's meaning and purpose for stakeholders, especially employees. It describes the desired long-term results of your company's efforts.*

He remembered the bewilderment that began to overwhelm him as he saw the word 'purpose' included in the definition of a vision. On returning to his MBA notes, the only further elucidation he could find was that such statements were better if they were short. Indeed, the shorter the better. Classic was the old Federal Express version: *Absolutely, positively, overnight.* Then there was the Komatsu versus Caterpillar battle for heavy construction equipment, where Komatsu had coined the phrase: *Get Caterpillar.* Others were longer, such as the one from Dunkin Donuts: *We strive to keep you at your best, and we remain loyal to you, your tastes and your time.*

Not sure how any of those help, and what had 'striving to keep you at your best' got to do with doughnuts? he had thought at the time. And indeed, still found odd. He remembered thinking that his first attempt had been short and identified key targets. However, he hadn't been sure of the emotional appeal or the extent to which it was inspirational. His second attempt, which he remembered very well as it was also the version he took forward, had tried to rectify those deficiencies:

> "*Our mission and vision over the next three years is to be one of the leading suppliers of solar and solar-related technology to both residential and commercial customers, that will enable them to live better and more fulfilling environmental and economic lives. Our focus will initially be the UK, and our purpose is profitable growth.*"

He was still quite pleased with this as it covered everything in one statement, but was still restricted to two sentences. He had felt that it would appeal to the greener elements in the market, as well as providing a good starting point for sales conversations. At the same time, it covered the 'mission' the Eternal Elements board had devolved to him: profitable growth. He had felt that there was little anyone could object to or be ashamed about when it was published more widely. He remembered imaging how it would look on a professional network blog post or other social media discussions. In the end, it had never reached these channels, but that had not been his fault.

He also recalled a different MBA session, where a speaker had differentiated between giving directions and creating direction. He remembered being somewhat confused about the difference. How could direction be created without giving directions? The session had emphasised the idea of getting people to think for themselves by asking questions. This had been referred to as the 'Socratic Method,' a term he liked to use as it reflected a sophistication that he felt was important for someone in his role. However, whenever he had tried to utilise the approach, people had always struggled to give the right answers, and he had always found that they were much happier when he had told them what they had to do. He remembered this had been exactly the case with his team-building exercise on his MBA. The session had also emphasised the need to start with the vision of the end goal and an idea of why it had been chosen.

'Well,' he had thought, *'my encapsulation of our mission, vision and purpose does exactly that.'* He had hoped that it would inspire people to think about their part in delivering the end result. He felt that it should also have solved any problems of choosing priorities. Looking back, he still felt that it was a good statement, even though it had not been immediately endorsed.

Having been through some other iterations, he had eventually returned to his second attempt, and deleted all his other efforts. He had then asked Annabel to organise another Strategy Away Day for the following week, where he would present the overarching statement of direction, and use breakout groups to explore the questions raised during the appraisal interviews.

Idly watching the swans, Toby wondered if he was the only person to have struggled with the difference between the concepts of vision, mission and purpose. The cynic in him thought they might be something dreamed up by consultancies to sell their services. It was, after all, a well-worn path.

Were there simpler ways of providing direction, or did it have to be complex out of necessity?

10

CREATING DIRECTION

Annabel had booked the same venue as the previous Away Day. It had similarly started with coffee and pastries on arrival. When everyone had poured their second cup, they had settled round the boardroom-style table, with Toby at the head with the screen behind him, and his laptop on the table in front of him. In the back of his mind, he was still thinking about the idea of direction, and its creation rather than the issuing of instructions. He still wasn't at all sure about the difference, and he toyed with the idea that this might be an opportunity to experiment.

However, as this was a Monday, he had started the meeting with updates from each attendee. He was pleased to note that the level of sniping had reduced from the earlier meetings, which he felt had been helped by Bob's efforts to mend fences between staff. He had also invited Albert, the trainee commercial/industrial salesperson, to attend this part of the meeting so that others could hear first-hand about progress in this area, and see the visual case-study he had created.

Albert had first taken them through the case-study, and then described the other successful contract that had now been installed, although neither were yet able to supply excess generation to the grid. This had led to Christina asking about the money.

"So, how much are they retaining? How long will this take? And how sure are we that they will be paying when they say they will?" she had asked. "It seems to me that there is no real end in sight, and from what I can gather from the figures you supplied, the retained money is just about equal to the profit due from each contract. Effectively, neither of these two initial contracts are showing a positive return. In fact, with the cost overruns, there's a question mark as to whether they will achieve a break-even position once the final payments have been made."

Toby had explained that this was normal in this sort of market, "What you've got to recognise, Christina, is that there is a learning curve to navigate, and some up-front investment is required in order to get to a position of profitability."

"Sorry, I hadn't meant to offend or question your understanding of the market, but I think these things have to be said."

'Better leave it at that,' Toby had thought. *'Don't want to get too embroiled in yet another awkward discussion.'*

Moving on to prospects, Albert had outlined some responses from the professional networks. He had managed to get meetings with two of the organisations that had shown an interest. They were both small. One was a school that needed a grant to progress an installation, but to apply for the grant, they needed a comprehensive 'bid' from three different suppliers. Bob had wondered whether it was worth the time and effort,

"Surely the successful bidder in that sector was likely to be the cheapest? Isn't there a problem if Eternal is 'navigating a learning curve', we are surely not in a position to compete on price?"

At that point, Ian had chipped in, "On the other hand, if that is a promising sector, and the market was worth it, would taking a loss-leader approach produce dividends in the longer run?"

"Good thoughts," Toby had responded. "Let's look at the other prospect and take it from there."

The other prospect was an independent hotel. Apart from not conforming to the ideal customer specification, installation would need to be carried out in the following January when the hotel shut for annual maintenance.

"Not an ideal time to be climbing about on an icy roof," Gilbert had interjected, "and why are you relying on professional networks? Surely some local advertising and mail-shots might get a better response? As you know, that's always worked without resorting to the hit-and-miss of social media."

"It's a question of focusing on those areas of the market that are most likely to be interested in using solar in the most cost-effective way," Toby had patiently explained. "We need to be concentrating on these networks as they will get us in direct contact with prospects that fit the profile of our ideal targets. Better than the hit-and-miss of mail-shots and local advertising." Toby had immediately regretted this last remark.

"Just like the school and hotel identified so far?"

"You're right," Toby had conceded, trying to take the tension he had potentially created out of the situation. "In fact, I was thinking that now might be the time to give responsibility for the professional networks to you, Gilbert. You might get some more positive returns than Albert here has had to date. Basically, we need more blog posts, and I think more direct communications with our ideal prospects are required."

'Was this creating direction?' Toby had wondered to himself. *'I didn't issue instructions, but just aired a view of what was needed. And I do hope Albert wasn't too offended.'*

"Well, that's a change in tune. I thought you had to be experiencing the hot breath of the customer to be able to use them!" Gilbert had retorted.

"Certainly for the initial phase, but with the pressure to get to as many prospects as possible, I think it's time to share the load," Toby had explained, hoping that this would pacify Gilbert.

"Not so easy when it all seems to be in your name. I did have a look a bit ago, but can't even log on without you by my side, and you seem to spend most of your time in your office with the door shut, or out on the road."

Recognising that this was going nowhere, Toby had indicated that they would pursue the conversation outside the meeting. A short discussion then spontaneously ensued about loss-leaders, learning curves, and communications media. Toby wondered if he was creating direction through this kind of debate even though he had not initiated it. There was some mention of the ideal customer and the different sectors that Toby had discussed, but he couldn't discern any conclusions emerging. If anything, he thought there was more confusion than clarity. *'No direction creation there,'* he said to himself.

In the end he had cut the discussion, and said that Albert had to push on with the contacts he had made and continue to get a foot-in-the-door with more prospects. The targets were clear and there was no real room for debate about learning curves and the like. The important thing was not to stand still, but to grasp the opportunities as they appeared. Time for a coffee break and a 'thank you' to Albert for coming along.

After coffee, it was time to reveal the new statement of mission and vision. He had first described, as best he could, the need for such statements, in spite of his own confusion, and the value of providing motivation for people.

"Basically, I need everyone round the table to now use the statement as a beacon for people to follow." With that, he had beamed the statement onto the screen. "So, let's all share our thoughts about the meaning of the statement. Any questions?" He shuddered a bit as he recalled the silence that had followed. "All clear then? In which case, it's time for the breakout groups. We'll take an hour, and then I'd like you to return with a plan for how you will use the statement to focus people's minds."

Toby had asked Ian to bring along one of his senior salespeople to even up the numbers so that they could work in three pairs. He had put Gilbert with Bob, as he thought Bob would be the best person to keep Gilbert under control, and prevent him from 'going off on one'. Christina was with Edith, as they worked together on some areas, and Ian went with his senior salesperson. On return, and after tea and cakes, they had reported back. Toby nominated Ian to go first.

"Myself and my colleague here think that if we start all our group sales meetings with the statement displayed on a screen, it would soon become embedded in the minds of the whole team. We think this should apply to all meetings whether they are in person or virtual."

"Sounds like a good way forward," agreed Toby, "anything else?"

"Yes. We thought it would be good to incorporate it in the sales literature we use when we come to reprint. Our only concern was the inclusion of the term 'profitable growth.' We wondered if that might make us look a bit grasping, or give the impression that we might be a bit aggressive?"

Seeing an opportunity to employ the Socratic approach, Toby had responded with, "What do the rest of you guys think?" After some discussion, they came to the conclusion that it should be excluded.

"Look," Toby had had to explain, "the Eternal positioning of 'the original solar panel company' is there to give the impression of depth, but needs a dynamic narrative to ensure it isn't seen as sleepy. I think people would prefer to deal with a company that has ambition, than one that is seen as just sitting around in a self-satisfied sort of way." (*'Trust them to come up with the wrong answer,'* he recollected.)

"What about the idea that part of Eternal's appeal is its size and family nature?" Bob had wondered. "Perhaps looking like we are nakedly after growth could make people feel that we might become more remote or anonymous?"

"I think that size will equate to stability in people's minds," Toby had countered, "and, of course, this will be particularly significant for the commercial/industrial markets. It's unlikely that they would want to engage with a supplier they felt might be gone in a couple of years. Trust me, I have quite a bit of experience in this sector. I think we need to move on. What about you, Christina and Edith?" he had said, not feeling quite so positive.

Toby was conscious that he had isolated the two women, and wondered whether it would have been better to share them around, but he couldn't see either of them working well with Gilbert, or at least being able to corral him - especially Edith. They would probably wind each other up into some sort of frenzy.

Christina presented their thoughts, "We both felt that we could get the statement printed on some attractive posters and place them in prominent positions around the building. I've seen other motivational posters work in some of my previous companies, and we could see it working here. After all, it would liven up the décor, given that most notices are health and safety based."

"I saw one the other day that has lingered with me," Edith added, "*With God, all things are possible,* it said. I don't know, it just hit me as a very uplifting message and, as we're dealing with a mission, I thought it would work for us. I've always felt that there was not enough thought around spirituality in business, and that people would recognise that there is lots they could achieve. Mr Burkinshaw - the NED, and I, both agree on that."

Toby wasn't sure quite how motivational that would be, and hoped the Eternal posters would be more focused. Nervously, he turned finally to Bob and Gilbert.

"I think Gilbert and I had a good discussion," ventured Bob. "We didn't necessarily agree on everything, but a bit of exploring the territory can be very useful. Gilbert here, in fact, expressed a few concerns, but had some positive ideas about how the statement could be amended."

"I think we all know that Gilbert is never short of an opinion," Toby found himself saying, and again, immediately regretted it. "Carry on."

"Well, Gilbert concluded that he would be happy to include an amended version as a postscript to emails, along with all the other footnotes about wrongly addressed emails etc. He would also get it on to flyers and direct mail."

Feeling uncomfortable, and hoping to avoid another public confrontation, Toby addressed Bob directly, "And what do you think of that as a way forward, Bob?"

"Well," replied Bob cautiously, "I think Gilbert has to be comfortable with what he puts in his comms. His suggestion was not too far away from the one we've been discussing, so maybe we should give it an airing?"

Was this all part of creating direction, Toby wondered? With some trepidation, he had agreed to let the team have a look. Gilbert's suggestion was:

> *"Over the next three years we will remain a family business and a leading supplier of solar-related technology, mainly to residential, but also to some commercial customers at good prices for all".*

"Much less wordy and to the point," Gilbert had cut in. "And I still believe that price is our major 'foot-in-the-door' appeal, so we need to have that as a prominent part of the statement. Frankly, people can't be bothered to read something longer. And while we're at it, I can see the point, but I'm not totally convinced we need anything like this. A recent speaker at the Chamber of Commerce on 'Down to Earth Business,' demonstrated that for SMEs such as us, we don't really need what he called, 'Business School Mumbo Jumbo.' We just need to get on with things."

"An interesting way of looking at things," Toby had responded. "Something to think about. Good effort on the statement though, Gilbert." Reluctant to throw it open to the team as it might become contentious, he went on, "It perhaps loses some of the 'green' appeal we were trying to include, but the idea of introducing the 'family' nature of the business may have some merit."

Hoping that this would appease Gilbert, he then offered to report back at a later date, knowing that he was not going to allow Gilbert to sabotage his efforts. Gilbert nodded sourly, and the meeting moved on. *'Well,'* Toby had thought, *'that has probably done some direction creation if nothing else. It must be clear to everyone what the direction of travel is from now on, maybe even Gilbert.'*

The rest of the meeting was setting out a series of 'to do' lists and exchanging notes on where to get what, what font to use, and the best place for posters etc. Feeling much better, Toby had then drawn the meeting to a close with a few warm words of encouragement. He had thanked them for their efforts, noted a good team spirit, and the new dual focus for the future growth of the business.

The next step was to make the presentation to the board, now that the team had been informed. He paused for a moment to reconsider whether he should have let the board know first, but at the time had decided that while board approval would have given him more purchase with the SMT, it had needed them behind it to make the board think well of it. He had invited Albert, the trainee commercial salesperson along, as the exposure would be good for him, and he had used the same rationale for the board before the big reveal. Hoping for a better response than the silence that had greeted the statement at the SMT Away Day, he asked for questions and comments. Sure enough, there were a lot of questions.

"What did the initial contracts with commercial customers teach you?"

"How are you going to organise operations to serve the extra markets you want us to move into?"

"Why are you restricting us to the UK? What about Ireland, if nowhere else?"

"Where does our usual price offer fit? Surely this is the most effective way to get a 'foot-in-the-door'?"

"Is it wise to publish our desire for profitable growth? Doesn't it make us look too commercial?"

And from Christina, "Have you calculated the cost of what is effectively a rebranding?"

'Where's the team spirit from Christina?' Toby had inwardly moaned. She hadn't said anything about rebranding in the meeting, why bring this up now? Trying to impress the rest of the board he supposed.

The board had then discussed the statement, and came to the conclusion that it was okay for internal consumption in the form presented, but were concerned about the profitable growth angle on more public forums. In the end, they had decided that it could be used on emails and printed matter, but not on social media, where there was more likelihood of a backlash. Feeling that he had defended his position well, Toby was disappointed that he would be barred from what he thought was their most powerful communications channel, but knew he was on a sticky wicket if he argued further. Although Christina was in the meeting, Albert had left, and so Toby thought it best not to mention the defeat to the rest of the SMT unless it came up in conversation.

Toby's next move was to break the news to Gilbert that he had to stick with the original statement minus the profitable growth sentence. He had dreaded the smug look he knew he would get. He had also wondered whether a more acceptable 'purpose' could be created, as his instinct told him that a business without a purpose is the weaker for it. Anyway, with a week's leave due, he recalled that it would give him time to have a good think.

In fact, thinking had not got him very much further forward, and looking at the swans with their simple focus on feeding and breeding, he wondered whether he had been making things too complicated.

Business did that for you, he mused. Could I have simplified things? Perhaps, but I can't think how.

11

A COACHING CONVERSATION

By now, Toby was approaching the end of his first year, and felt he deserved the week's leave. He had taken Sally away for a long weekend, and as he had promised himself, he had a good think. He had not only reflected (fruitlessly) on purpose, but also the difficulties he had experienced in establishing himself at Eternal. There was quite a list, but top amongst them was:

- Gilbert Turkey
- Edith Smallie
- The lack of financial information
- The almost dysfunctional SMT
- Influencing the board.

Pondering on them, he remembered a mentor he had worked with during his MBA, and wondered whether a bit of executive coaching might help sort out some of the issues he faced. Many of the business blogs he followed had recommended it. Going online, he found a plethora of coaching outfits and individuals offering their services, but eventually found a register of qualified people and some recommendations. Picking one that looked as if they understood the world of SMEs, he made an appointment.

Session one was apparently for 'testing the chemistry' and agreeing the 'coaching contract' between them (which he thought sounded a bit airy-fairy) as well as outlining the issues he wanted to talk about. The coach had made him pick his most important one as a starting point, which he had found hard. With the help of the coach, he eventually picked the SMT. If he could get them working better together, that could help solve some of his other issues. For their second session the following week, the coach had tasked him with identifying what the problems were. Although he would be back at work, he was sure he would be able to slip away for a couple of hours for this.

Leaving work for his second meeting after saying he was going to the dentist, he realised he hadn't thought much about the SMT issues. Instead, he used the drive to come up with a few things. Three, he thought, would be enough. These he had presented to the coach.

"First are the two family members that work for me, but I think wield undue influence with the Eternal board. Surely this is an abuse of their position, and the board should recognise that they need to stop them going over my head, as it clearly undermines my position? Second, is the outright insubordination from Gilbert Turkey. He constantly challenges me in open forums i.e. the SMT meetings, and in private is downright antagonistic. He's obviously jealous of my position and feels he should have had my job. What he doesn't see is that he's just useless. Third, is the seeming inability of the SMT as a whole to see the bigger picture, or for individuals to contribute to meetings in anything more than a trivial way. They just seem reluctant to get involved or to put their head above the parapet. They all need to shape up and start taking their responsibilities seriously, the board included."

"How do the family connections affect the ability of the SMT to function more effectively?" asked the coach.

"In a number of ways. Their presence clearly inhibits discussion, as everyone knows that if anything derogatory is said about the board, it would get straight back to them. In addition, they are perfectly capable of putting a spin on things that could set the board against me and the agreements I'd made with the SMT, which would undermine me. Indeed, there are several examples of the board blocking or limiting initiatives I had proposed to them. Finally, they clearly feel secure in their positions as family members, and that emboldens them in the way they act. Edith is hard to shift from her position on customer service and, as stated, Gilbert is just downright rude. He observably affects the atmosphere in the meetings."

"So, what do you think their motivations are?" the coach had then asked.

"To my mind, it's clear that Gilbert is just a nasty piece of work, and Edith retains a misplaced loyalty to Hamish."

"Any other motivations that might be at play?"

"What else could be going on?"

"Well, what about the fact that there are obvious family connections; they all know each other and have a shared history. In addition, they must attend events outside the business where they would naturally talk about the business. Could it be that they just want to be helpful or harbour a desire to be influential? Maybe they just find it difficult to cope with change, or find it hard to trust outsiders. Do you think they might even harbour doubts about your good self?"

Toby hadn't liked these questions and thought them a bit petty, especially the last suggestion, so he stuck to his point that they needed to recognise their responsibilities. Moving on, and recognising that Toby was becoming quite defensive, the coach had gently asked about the SMT meetings in general.

"The problem is, that when we get to talk about important things like the diversification into the commercial/industrial markets, they never seem to have anything to say. They don't ask questions or make comments, even though I give them ample room to express opinions and make challenges. I welcome challenges. I remember reading about a CEO that didn't invite challenge, and how it was his Achilles heel and his downfall. No, I welcome challenge, but never get anything meaningful. Just a whole load of sniping questions."

"That clearly annoys you. But why do you think there might be no worthwhile challenge?"

At this point, Toby remembered feeling as if they were going round in circles. Plainly, the presence of the family members was an inhibition, and maybe the rest were just a little limited in their thinking. He remembered feeling the flush of anger that had emerged during the conversation, but wasn't quite sure how to interpret it, even now.

"Before we finish," the coach had gone on, "we should perhaps spend a little time on the board, as you mentioned it in your initial list. I was wondering what you thought their role was?"

"Three main functions," replied Toby. "First is to approve the decisions of the CEO and the SMT, second is to endorse the strategy, and third is to decide on the dividends."

"And what about governance?" the coach had asked.

"What about it?"

"Well, who's role is it to oversee the risks in the business and to ensure decisions are in the best interests of the company and wider stakeholders?"

"I think that is the responsibility of the CEO with the support of the SMT. It's our job to look carefully at the decisions we make, the strategy we develop, and the long-term security of the business. That's what we are there for, isn't it? And therein lies the problem; the rest of the SMT don't seem capable of living up to those expectations."

"I'm not sure everyone would agree with that view of governance. Let's discuss it another time."

The coach had then asked about how board meetings went. Toby explained that the chair sent out an agenda, they all arrive in the board room, and the chair would conduct the meetings, "Nothing unusual there," Toby had suggested.

"What happens at the end?" the coach had asked.

"We all get up and return to our various tasks and offices," he replied, trying to hide the sarcasm he felt.

"No tea, coffee, pre or post meeting socialising? No chance to lobby or discover what people were thinking? No development of rapport with individual board members?"

"No, the chair is ex-military, and doesn't go in for that sort of thing."

"And have you ever suggested it?"

"Not sure it's my place to make that sort of suggestion. Not part of the culture for board meetings," responded Toby.

"Find it difficult to challenge?"

With that the session had run out of time and the coach drew the discussion to a close with one last question, "And if I was to ask you, what you felt your role in all this was; what you have done to overcome these problems, how would you answer? So far it seems you feel like you are being battered from all sides by external issues and forces. I think the question for you, Toby, is what should *you* be doing about these issues? Something for us to talk about next time, eh?"

Toby had paid for the session and then taken his leave. He had thought about using the company credit card, but decided that he'd like to keep this under wraps. He didn't want people to think he was in trouble or in need of therapy.

On the way back to work, he decided that the coach had been unnecessarily antagonistic, with a lot of implied criticism. Well, he hadn't gone there to be attacked. He'd gone for help and some useful suggestions; some tips and techniques for handling the issues. He hadn't wanted this incessant questioning without much useful advice. It was clear he really didn't understand Toby's situation.

On returning to the office, he cancelled the forthcoming sessions and drew a line under any further attempts to get coaching support. The MBA mentor had been much more helpful, pointing him in the right direction for some of his assignments, and providing a few thoughts about how he could improve things. Coaching was evidently *not* up to the hype that everyone gave it.

Time to get on with things, he had said to himself, ironically parroting the quote Gilbert had used from his Chamber of Commerce speaker. Next was another look at the commercial/industrial markets, another chat with Gilbert about the professional networks, a further chat with Edith - although she was now on holiday, and a look at the sales figures and accounts that were finally emerging from Christina's machinations.

In spite of his disappointment with his coaching experience, Toby found that the questions the coach had asked had lingered with him. What was governance all about? Had he been too limited in his thinking about the family dynamics? What were people's motivations? And what had been his role in all this? Perhaps there was more to coaching than he had thought.

Anyway, none of this mattered now, as two weeks later, the chairman had called him into his office and summarily fired him.

12

THE RIDE HOME

By now the pub was emptying, and Toby felt it was time to call home for a lift and to face the music. He paid for his food and drink and got some change for the payphone in the corner.

"Hello, darling, it's only me. I'm afraid I need a favour. I'm at the pub by the river in the village and need a lift home. Any chance you could come and pick me up?"

"Where's the car?" she had asked. "Or are you over the limit again?"

"No, no. Nothing like that, just haven't got the car with me."

"Oh no! You haven't had an accident, have you?"

"No. It's all okay. I'll explain when you get here."

"I'll be about 20 minutes; can you start walking? I need to be back for a call before 2.15?"

Toby considered the idea of carrying his golf clubs and back pack for a mile or so, and thought better of it, "Easiest if you can come to the pub if that's okay?"

"Oh, all right. Are you hurt? Are you sure you haven't had an accident? What are you hiding?" came the slightly irritated response.

"I'm fine. As I said, I'll explain everything when you get here. Nothing to worry about," he said, conscious that he was really stretching the truth by now.

Sally duly arrived twenty minutes later, and was rather perplexed to see him load his golf clubs into the boot of the family Skoda. As he settled into his seat, Sally immediately began to quiz him again.

"So, what's going on? Why have you got your golf clubs and no car?" and after a pause, "You've been sacked, haven't you? I told you things were not looking too healthy for you at Eternal. It's true, isn't it?"

"I prefer to think of it as being released to move on to pastures new," Toby had said, trying not to make it sound so harsh.

For the next ten minutes, Sally berated Toby for not listening to her and failing to address at least some of the issues that he had obviously been facing.

"Who sacked you? Must have been the chairman. I don't know how many times I've said that you need to put more effort into building a relationship with him. He's clearly the driving force in that business. I know you keep saying that he's a cold fish and doesn't welcome friendly advances, but some of the others seem to get on with him okay. From what you say, Hamish certainly did. And then there's Edith and Gilbert. With all your 'relationship skills', you must have been able to develop something better than the fraught exchanges you've reported to me. This is a family business, and they are family, and very likely to take precedence over a new person from outside, no matter how tedious the rest of the family found them. I think the chairman indicated that to you on a number of occasions.

And then there was all that fuss you made over 'creating direction.' I told you that you needed to make sure that people understood what you wanted; unless you didn't really understand what it was that you really wanted! Was that it? Was it you that was struggling to clarify what people should be doing? Or was it them? People take a long time to take new ideas on board, and often have to be told several times.

And that's just the half of it." she concluded.

Toby had become monosyllabic in his responses, conscious that there might be a few home truths in what she was saying. In spite of his mood, he was slightly amused by the fact that they were literally 'home truths.' But that didn't take anything away from the fact that he could not ignore the truth that, somehow, he had screwed up. And from what the chairman had said so plainly, it was all about his leadership.

"And what was the pay off?" Sally asked at last.

"Just the final month, although knowing them, they'll probably only give me the last two weeks, not even the whole month. Penny-pinching lot. Too focused on dividends and lining their own pockets. Not sure I stood a chance," he had grumbled.

"That's a shame as we're very tight for money at the moment too. So, the good news is that I've just been provisionally offered a job. That's why I need to be back for 2.15, as my potential new boss is going to give me a call to get an answer to one more question to confirm the offer, and then to take me through the induction process. Thank goodness one of us is on the ball!"

"Oh, that's great Sally. Something at the library or Citizens Advice? Admin assistant, or what?"

"Nothing like that actually. I've been offered the job of library manager at the specialist art library attached to the university in town. It's 20 full-time equivalent staff and £43K a year."

"How on earth did you get that?" asked Toby, trying to hide the disbelief in his voice.

"Well, I've always been interested in art, as you know. And I've often popped in there after dropping the kids in town. After a while, I started nosing around to work out how things worked and who the movers and shakers were. Eventually, I connected with the director of library services, and she invited me to apply, knowing my interests and library experience. They definitely did *not* want a qualified librarian, but someone that could bring an external perspective. My CIPD and HR experience also helped of course."

"Well done," was the most Toby could say, still trying to comprehend what was going on.

"So, here's the question," Sally went on, "they asked me to think about the most important quality I needed to bring to the job, and to be prepared to clarify it with the director this afternoon. I know what I want to say, but what would be your take on it?"

Toby was silent for a while, reflecting on his recent experiences, and then with a deep sigh whispered, "Avoiding the deadly sins of leadership I suppose!"

EPILOGUE

INTERVIEW TRANSCRIPTS WITH KEY PEOPLE

Annabel (PA to Toby)

I hear all the gossip. Everyone knows that I'm very discreet, so they never got anything inappropriate from me all the time I was working for Hamish. I knew so much about what was going on but never breathed a word to anyone. For instance, I was the first to know that Hamish was going to retire, and only the chairman and me know the real reasons why. Lots of people suspected it was the drink, but no-one really knew. Hamish had been under a lot of pressure from the family and the board to explain the strategy for the business, but had found it increasingly difficult to do so. He'd introduced a lot of initiatives, but knew they were steadily losing margin and was at a loss to know what to do about it. There were 'too many choices,' as he kept saying to the chairman. That's what really did for him.

All this led to stress and him hitting the bottle earlier and earlier in the day. He used to call it a little 'sharpener,' but I'm not sure how sharp it made him. I was replenishing the drinks cabinet ever more frequently. As it was paid for from the petty cash, no one else really knew, and it was easy to slip things past poor old Paul Travers. The last straw was when he was pulled over for drink-driving. They kept it out of the papers as it was not local, but the board and all the family became aware of the problem. After that, his wife issued an ultimatum: *"Sort yourself out or I'm off,"* and she'd seek injunctions to keep him away from the grandchildren. Turns out that drink didn't help him much at all, so he was going to lose out in every way if he carried on.

Once he'd made the decision to leave, things got a lot better, and they appointed Toby. I mean, Hamish is well-off, so they decided to move to a place on the coast in France originally owned by his father, where they could indulge their love of sailing and have somewhere nice for the rest of the family to visit. He also joined Alcoholics Anonymous, which I think has helped a lot. Anyway, they seem much happier now. It's a shame he didn't recognise the need to get some help with the business earlier; someone who could do the things he couldn't. Hamish had a tendency to want to be a 'real' leader – leading the charge with everyone excited and cheering behind him. I have to say, the chairman encouraged that sort of behaviour, but I'm not sure it helped that much. So, in the end, he tried to do everything himself.

The trouble with Toby was that he had some of the same characteristics. He saw himself as 'the big cheese,' and tended to want to do things his way. He was always trying to push his ideas onto people; to persuade them of the merits of what he was proposing, not always successfully. From my perspective, he often gave in too easily. I think he may have been too concerned with what people thought of him. At least he didn't keep coming up with a new initiative every other week like Hamish used to. It was the devil's own job to keep track of the changes Hamish kept introducing.

Toby also spent a lot of time in his office with the door shut. Who knows what he was working on, but it certainly didn't involve me. Not even sure he trusted me that much, even though he was a little over-familiar at times. Still, I've been dealing with men all my life so it was never a problem. But I never really got a chance to show just how trustworthy I am! I was always reminding him of some of the projects he had initiated that needed following up, but in the end, I stopped, as he didn't seem to welcome the prompts.

Every few days or so, he'd emerge from his office and walk round the building chatting to people. With the men he talked about F1, golf, and football. With the women he'd ask about their children and holidays. He spent much more time with the men than the women. He called it MBWA, which I think means Management By Wandering Around. I'm not sure how much the staff felt comfortable with him trying to 'make a connection' with them. They were never sure what he was trying to do or why he was doing it.

This all seemed to encourage people to confide in me. *They* think they can trust me and that I have the ear of the CEO, and that perhaps their concerns will get through to him if they tell me. Little do they know that he never asked me anything about what was going on, or what the general mood was. I could have told him so much.

Hamish Smalley (Departed CEO)

Frankly, I was struggling to take the business forward. I'd doubled the turnover in my ten years, but couldn't seem to get profits to do the same. Paul Travers, the accountant, was one of the old-fashioned finance people, and not great at providing any analysis, but the rest of the family all seemed to value him and I didn't have the heart to oust him. He'd been with the business a long time – I inherited him from my father after Paul's father had died. Whether his figures were accurate or not, I don't really know, but the auditors always signed off the accounts eventually, although they were often late. The one thing I really admired about Toby was his removal of Paul. He was clearly out of his depth, and Toby managed it very well, even though it cost us a pound or two. Inevitable if we weren't going to make a big song and dance about him going, which could have backfired by unsettling other long-servers.

Anyway, having been done for drink-driving in the Lake District, I knew the writing was on the wall, and to save my marriage and reputation, I told the chairman my time was up. Toby was clearly the best of the candidates we saw, and I could see a lot of myself in him. Good for continuity, I thought. And he certainly seemed to understand the market and leadership; perhaps the leadership I had been unable to provide. The handover was very perfunctory: the chairman wanted a clean break and for Toby to make his own assessments and decisions. Besides, the staff had been kept in the dark, and I didn't want to be seen to be 'hanging around'.

I come back for all the board meetings and try to give myself three or four days to catch up with old acquaintances like the old operations manager, who retired at the same time as me, and some chums at the golf club. I also needed to keep up my AA attendance. It also gives me the opportunity to devote time to board papers, and I always spend time with the chairman. It had taken some time to get to know him, but once you got past his militaristic exterior, he was much easier to talk to. It was always good to catch up with Annabel too. I hadn't realised when I was CEO just what a valuable source of information she is.

Toby was always well presented and certainly looked the part of a CEO. His presentations were consistently professional, and he had some good ideas for expanding the business. Although his analysis was excellent, the reason he was restricted in his proposal to expand into the commercial/industrial sector was because the finances were not necessarily clear, and the payback some way off. He knew that the dividends were almost sacrosanct, and that money for investment had to come from improved profits. In this case, the egg came first! In retrospect, I don't know why he didn't understand that profits had to come before investment was possible. We had expected him to concentrate on existing markets, and to use his undoubtedly excellent sales skills to accelerate our growth there. It was a surprise when he proposed diversification so early.

Towards the latter part of his first year, I had increasing numbers of people seeking me out for 'confidential' conversations. Not many, but enough to raise a few worries. Their concerns were around the direction of the business. They could see that the business needed to expand, but they were not so sure of their priorities. And they had found it difficult to give that feedback to Toby. He was either away, locked in his office, or dismissive of their questions. Of course Gilbert had little time for him, having wanted his job, but he isn't stupid, and Edith reported that Toby made her feel uncomfortable by always pushing her to change the way we had worked so successfully together. We both knew there were two types of customers, and the moaners were not going to do us any good - no matter what we did for them.

In the end, neither myself, the chairman, nor Mr Burkinshaw (our external non-exec, who is a good judge of character) understood what Toby's agenda was in terms of leading the business. Again, a bit similar to myself I suppose! He had clearly lost the support of the staff, and profits didn't seem to be going in the right direction. In addition, he looked as if the stress was getting to him as he desperately defended the diversification into the commercial/industrial markets. Collectively we decided to move on, and put Bob Meadows in as interim CEO.

Sally Thunder (Toby's wife)

Toby is an excellent salesman and a hard worker; well, he always tells me he's a hard worker! He could sell snow to the Eskimos, if you know what I mean. He was very excited when Eternal offered him the post of CEO. He felt he had been preparing for such a role for some time, so it was very disappointing when he was sacked, in my opinion quite brutally, after only a year. No written or final warnings, or anything. I had suspected things were not going well, but Toby disagreed and said I just didn't understand, and was worrying for nothing.

One thing that seemed strange to me was that in his previous roles, Toby had been a great networker, but at Eternal, he seemed to become a bit of a lone wolf. I suppose salespeople often are. Clearly, relations with Gilbert Turkey and Edith Smalley were not easy, and that Paul Travers was a bit of a dinosaur. But I always felt he should have put more effort in with the chairman. He was the power behind the throne, so to speak, and likely to be a key influencer of the board. He would often refer to organisational politics, and said that he was never going to enter that arena. He didn't play political games like some people. Toby had therefore also shunned contact with Hamish claiming he didn't trust him and questioned what he could learn from him given his record in the business.

"Turnover is vanity. Profit is sanity", he'd quote at me. *"And there was a lot of turnover but not much sanity under Hamish"*. The same applied to the external non-exec, whom he

dismissed as a 'bit of a fuddy-duddy'. I had met him once and thought there might be more to him than met the eye. But that is also typical of Toby; I feel that he often undervalues people, including me sometimes, even though we get on well most of the time. We really do enjoy each other's company. I think his tendency to undervalue people stems from his early experiences when people undervalued him, and he had to work very hard to maintain any self-esteem. I know he finds it hard to trust people, and is always suspicious that they are looking down on him or trying to make fun of him.

What was also strange was that Toby seemed to understand a lot about leadership from his studies, plus his reading and his experiences of working under a fair few managers, both good and bad. And he led some very successful sales teams. However, when it came to being CEO at Eternal, he seemed to find it hard to put much of it into practice. I heard whispers in the town that Eternal was not a very happy place these days. Apparently, there was grumbling about some loyal and long-serving senior staff that were being badly treated, and some uncertainty about where they were going.

Basically, I think Toby was either trying to do the same job as he'd done before, or he was trying to be what he thought a CEO should be, but found his approach didn't work with all the issues he bumped into at Eternal. With his sales teams, he could always see the market better than them and point them to profitable opportunities. He was good at motivational messaging and negotiating targets. At heart, he was one of them, and they recognised that, and his skill in closing a deal.

I'm not sure at Eternal that they saw him as 'one of them,' and that threw him.

I'm also not sure being a CEO is about rules, tools, and techniques that you simply learn and then put into practice. He was always looking for a solution that he could use with the issues he faced. However, my HR training emphasised that we needed to look at people as individuals with different needs, motivations, and ways of working. After all, Churchill didn't seem to follow a rule book, and neither did Mandela or Obama. And what about Steve Jobs, and that Tim Cook at Apple? But what do I know?

Anyway, I have my own challenges ahead of me now. My first senior manager role with more than a couple of staff to manage. I hope I fare better than Toby, but you never know!

The Chairman – Non-Exec Leader of the Board

It was basically my decision to appoint Mr Thunder, although the key members of the board all agreed i.e. Hamish and Mr Burkinshaw, the external non-exec. The one naysayer was Paul Travers. However, he hadn't liked any of the candidates we saw. What impressed me most was Thunder's understanding of leadership and analysis of the market. Of course, we all thought diversification would probably need to wait, as there was no real money or scope for investment in new markets until profits improved. Besides, I'd always been given to understand that the first place to look for growth was to focus on your existing products in existing markets. There are plenty of residential properties without panels to be addressed first. It was therefore surprising that his first proposal was for diversification into the commercial/industrial sector. In the end we went along with it, as he was so sure it was the best way to achieve our goal of profitable growth.

Having been a Lieutenant Colonel in the Royal Signals, I have some experience of leadership. The army emphasises the need for the development of trust between leaders and subordinates, combined with guidance, empowerment, and the establishment of team goals. Hamish had problems in many of these areas, especially the latter. For Hamish, there was never a bad time for a new idea. I had encouraged him to think and act more like a leader; to get more focus; inspire people more, but he struggled to have authority with the staff. Mr Thunder was a bit similar. I'm not sure how much the staff trusted him or understood his motivations, and

I do feel that his efforts to empower them really meant leaving them to their own devices.

One problem seemed to be his habit of trying to engage with staff by MBWA, as he called it. Somehow, this didn't enable him to connect with the staff as he had hoped. In addition, he spent a lot of time shut away in his office, which didn't really help. I don't think he ever really engaged with the staff at more than a superficial level; there was always a distance. His requirement for a special parking spot only served to emphasise the gap between himself and the other employees. Now, being too close to staff is not good, but being too distant is also problematic.

I remember I once asked him what his agenda was when he went on his little tours of the building. I was hoping he would talk about establishing rapport, gathering information, assessing atmosphere, or ensuring they understood the direction he was charting for the business. What he said was that he just wanted to show them that he was a 'man-of-the-people,' rather than some posh bloke lauding it over them. It was a disappointing answer. I think he needed to be liked more than was appropriate for the job. He certainly didn't like looking like a fool.

Another issue was his demonstrable difficulty dealing with awkward people. It was obvious to all that he and Mr Turkey were at war with each other, which unfortunately was conducted in public on occasion, and he always seemed to deflect rather than address the issue. It's a shame that he didn't take the same approach as he had with Paul Travers. He would have found a lot of support in the board for his removal, even with Hamish.

When it came to the appraisals, again, I felt he missed an opportunity to let people know where they stood, and address the need for guidance and empowerment. Hamish had been similarly weak, and had over-graded most people. Mr Thunder seems to have carried on this tradition. I have often wondered why he didn't use his undoubted qualities more, or whether he was just bad at having difficult conversations; or maybe there was something deeper. After all, he put a lot of effort into impression management. Maybe he just didn't like losing face. Odd for a salesperson.

I know that as a leader, one cannot have close friendships with subordinates and as CEO, or indeed, as chairman of the board, friends at work are difficult to discipline or sack. However, Mr Thunder never even tried to develop a working relationship with myself or Hamish. I know I can be seen as austere and a bit distant, but I think I respond well if people make an effort. Chairmen are traditionally there to help the CEO navigate the pitfalls of the role, and I'm sure we could have avoided some of the difficulties Mr Thunder faced, but I never really got the opportunity.

All in all, we had to make a decision as to whether we cut our losses, or gave Mr Thunder more time to prove himself. The nail in his coffin was when Mr Burkinshaw said that he couldn't see him turning things around, and the newly available sales and financial figures did not bode well. We had been impressed with Mr Meadows, so we thought that at least we had a safe pair of hands while we decided what to do next. I don't like sacking people, but in the end, it was my responsibility, especially as I had championed his appointment in the first place.

Bob Meadows – Operations Manager

I knew Toby from a previous job where we were both employed by the same company. I was in a similar role to that on offer at Eternal, and Toby was certainly a good salesman back then. He had a small team of 4 sales personnel, and as is often typical of salespeople, they were all very self-contained, preferring to work on their own rather than as a team; Toby included. Toby managed the bigger accounts, and would agree targets with the sales team, develop training plans, and write reports for the board, which were basically summaries of the previous period's sales figures with some appropriate analysis. He was good at analysis, closing deals, and pacifying irate customers. He was also good at providing explanations when sales didn't accord with expectations. It's hard to understand why he didn't use some of his undoubted talents more in his CEO role. He'd done his MBA by then, which in my opinion had only really increased his ability to talk, what I call, 'business bollocks.' Sounds good but says little. In my book, an MBA stands for: Master of Bugger All.

When Toby phoned about the opportunity at Eternal, I was ready for a move. We'd just got a new MD, and I didn't much care for him. He had a distinct philosophy, and everyone understood what he wanted, which in reality was more than over-ambitious. Typical American in my book. Head office used to swoop in, poop on everyone, and then fly out again. Seagull management I've heard it called. I had hoped that Toby would be more flexible, realistic, and have some achievable priorities for us. He was certainly flexible, maybe too much so, but sadly, it was difficult to get a good understanding of where to focus. I'm not too sure how realistic he was either.

Eternal was/is an interesting case. In many ways, a typical family business. In my experience, the important thing to do is establish relationships with key family members and identify the blockers to progress. In this case, Gilbert Turkey was a blocker, and hard to get to know. I suspect he was too full of resentment to be turned around, but he wasn't necessarily all bad. When I worked with him at the mission statement meeting, he could see the point, even though he didn't admit it, but needed to be convinced and have his views considered more seriously than Toby or Hamish had managed. I imagine that if he was listened to and allowed to vent his spleen, he might be more malleable. Well, let's hope so given recent developments!

The other sticking point is Edith. Fiercely loyal to Hamish, the ex-CEO, she found it very difficult to deviate from his way of doing things. I think it was something Toby should have sorted out, but he really doesn't like conflict, which also maybe explains his difficulties with Gilbert. He had a habit of backing away from awkward situations. I imagine it has something to do with his early life. Apparently, his parents used to row a lot, especially about his younger sister, so you can see how that might have scarred him.

Basically, as I see it, Toby should either have invested a lot more time with both Gilbert and Edith to try and turn them round, or got them dismissed as he had done so successfully with Paul Travers. However, to do the latter he needed to have better relationships with the chairman. To do the former, he needed to spend less time in his office or, more recently, on the road.

By now, you'll have recognised that I'm a very plain-speaking person, which I think is important for someone in charge of operations, or indeed, for anyone in a senior position. I've had feedback that this can make me appear a bit harsh or difficult to deal with. I recognise that this is probably true, so I've always tried to caveat my difficult conversations with an explanation of my motives, although I'm not sure people always listen. I think Toby could have done more of that himself.

I also think Toby struggled with feedback. He was very conscious of how people saw him, and liked to convey an impression of 'being in charge' and not looking stupid. This made him defensive, which of course meant that sometimes he did look stupid, which didn't help his cause at all. I believe that if he'd tried to use some of his undoubted strengths and work better with feedback, he might have gotten on a lot more successfully. I'm no psychologist, but I think that he was hampered by his desire to avoid conflict, as I mentioned earlier, but also by being made fun of at school. He never told me exactly how it happened, but he once confided that he had a very derogatory nickname at school, which could easily have left a few dark shadows.

Anyway, the challenges are all mine now, at least until the board decides what to do. My chance to put into practice all the things that I think Toby should have done!

Edith Smalley –
Office and Customer Service Manager

When the chairman called us all together and announced that Hamish was leaving (I think I knew him well enough to be on first name terms, and we *were* family) I wasn't exactly gobsmacked, but it wasn't what I was expecting. I knew that his family situation wasn't ideal, and I had been wondering if he was going part-time or something. So, when the chairman sprang the news that Hamish was leaving and that this person, Mr Thunder, was replacing him, I was quite taken aback.

First impressions of Mr Thunder were that he certainly looked the part and spoke well, in spite of his apparent mishap with a box when he addressed the rest of the staff after the chairman had introduced him. But after that, I found him a bit dogmatic, and perhaps overly assertive in his views about customer service. It's a job I have been doing for quite some time and I certainly feel as if I know what I'm doing. In conjunction with Hamish, we had developed an approach that has seemed to work well. Hamish was focused on internal costs, especially in the couple of years before he retired, and he was clear that disruption of routines led to increased costs and decreased efficiency. We therefore needed to keep disruption from customer complaints to a minimum.

Mr Thunder did not seem to understand this philosophy, and I was disappointed that he made no effort to explore how useful it had been. I know that I can dig my heels in if I feel pushed or bulldozered, so let's just say that our exchanges were not that comfortable. After years of dealing with the family's children, I've learned when to put your foot down, and when to let things go if you are to be successful. And I think this ability is why they employed me as office manager in charge of customer service. Mr Thunder had no appreciation of how useful I could be. I sometimes wondered if the fact that I was a woman had any bearing on his behaviour. He'd been a little bit teasing during our first encounters, which I did not welcome, and which in fact, made me feel a bit uncomfortable. Thankfully, that stopped quite quickly, after which he became more forceful.

His main idea seemed to be demoting me by making me report to the new operations manager, Mr Meadows. He seems to be a much different character, although our ideas are almost polar opposites in terms of customer service. However, he too can be a bit forceful, and I wouldn't want to get the wrong side of him. Overall, I can see no reason to either change the way I have been working, or change my position within the business. I've spoken to Hamish several times since he retired, and he agrees with me that sticking to what we know is probably the best course of action until there is good evidence that a change would be beneficial for the company.

I've also spoken quite extensively with Gilbert, who also agreed with me that these newbies shouldn't be allowed to just march in and start throwing their weight around before they had understood the way in which Eternal works. Everyone knows that Gilbert can be a bit hot-headed, but his heart is in the right place, and he is very keen to do well. I think he feels a need to prove himself now that he's married to Hamish's daughter. In many ways, he's just like a child that needs some help to mature. He's certainly not stupid, although his behaviour can make him appear so at times.

Overall, I think the board was right to get rid of Mr Thunder. I don't think he exactly covered himself in glory. He didn't treat Paul Travers particularly well, and you never really knew what he was thinking or what the strategy for growing the business was beyond moving into the commercial/industrial sectors. In my opinion, he didn't make a success of that, and went in a bit half-heartedly once the board had placed restrictions on what he could do. In any case, I was never sure how we were supposed to manage the two different sectors; and by that, I mean the residential sector and the commercial/industrial sectors, and what the balance was between the two. We occasionally talked about it at the SMT meetings, but I never came away fully understanding what we were supposed to do. But I suppose that's typical of a salesperson; just focused on doing a deal.

Christina Casey – New Finance Director

It was a bit of a surprise when Toby phoned me to talk about a board FD role at his new business. Firstly, I was surprised that he had remembered me, and secondly I was surprised that he was a CEO. Although, admittedly, we hadn't been in touch for quite some time, I'd always seen him as a salesman, with many of the unfortunate traits that often go with people in that profession (if you can call it a profession.) He was very good at analysis, although more at what I'd call a tactical rather than strategic level, which is another surprise given his experience. Apart from that, he was a bit of a ladies' man, but all mouth and no trousers, if you see what I mean. Harmless, but a bit wearing. I've seen CEOs like that before, you know; running off with their secretaries etc. And I know how much respect they lose. At least Toby didn't do that!

If I'm honest, I think that Toby was probably a bit of a male chauvinist. Certainly not misogynistic, but he didn't seem to see women as equals. In many ways, he undervalued people, but I think this applied more to women than men. He seemed to focus on their looks, rather than their business capabilities. Not helpful in my opinion.

Our main connection since we last worked together was LinkedIn, but I hadn't seen any posts from him; not even an excited announcement of his CEO role, as many people do. I'm not that big a fan of LinkedIn, or indeed social media in general, but Toby seemed to embrace it for his new employer, which was another surprise given that he didn't seem to use it much himself. As a bit of a sleepy family business, I'm not sure how much they had bought into the whole social media or virtual professional networks idea, but I'm sure they have their merits. Toby seemed to think that market conditions meant that it was a no-brainer, and the most cost-effective way of generating leads. Unfortunately, the state of the accounts meant that it was impossible to get any good data to support that assertion.

My biggest disappointment was that the job was not exactly as it had been sold to me. Typical of a salesman CEO I suppose. I had expected a family business embracing family values, and a finance job I could inherit seamlessly from a long-standing, now retired, finance director. It turned out that my predecessor had been removed rather than retired, the family were not that cosy, and the finance system was a mess to say the least. Added to that, I had uncooperative staff, who eventually fled the nest, and who actually caused me quite a lot of stress. I'm not good with other people's emotions; it's why I'm in the profession that I am, but by golly, I got a lot of emotional outpourings from them. It should have been me that went off with stress, not them!

Ian Long – Sales Manager

I've been with Eternal for about twenty years now. I joined when Angus and the old Mr Travers had just about established the business, with Angus going door-to-door, and the financials handled part-time by Paul's dad. I'd already got experience of door-to-door selling (double-glazing), but the need for a hard sell was a bit uncomfortable. Solar felt a bit more ethical, so I decided to give them a go. As a team, we were quite successful and soon started building a sales force. The government initiatives helped a lot in those days before austerity hit.

Anyway, Angus upped and died on us, followed by the old Mr Travers, which is when Paul took over the financials. He was nowhere near as good as his dad. I think he struggled from the word 'go'; I'd often see him still here at 9.00pm when I got back to the office after I'd done a long day on the road. I think it was a case of everyone thinking that everyone else wanted to keep Paul, when in fact, no-one did! Somebody once told me it was probably a classic case of the Abilene Paradox, but I never looked it up to find out if it was.

When Hamish took over the helm, things changed a bit. He was more entrepreneurial than his dad, probably too much so in my opinion. He pushed for growth and put a lot of pressure on me and the team to increase turnover, which we did with the help of third-party freelancers and resellers. The best referrals were from local or regional builders, plus kitchen and bathroom suppliers; at a fee of course! The nationals were a dead loss. Gilbert did quite a good job of generating leads, although the quality has dropped off in the last couple of years.

The trouble with Hamish was that in his desperation to grow sales, he kept introducing new ideas - particularly new approaches to selling. We've been through Challenger Selling, The Sandler Selling System, SPIN Selling, and SNAP Selling, to name a few. Too much chopping and changing. In the old days, solar panels were a hard sell, but they're easier now. Not easy, but easier. And it wasn't just in sales that he introduced changes, it was the same elsewhere in the business. Ironically, with Hamish's anxiety about costs, all the changes generated costs rather than saving anything. No real sense of stability.

So, when Toby arrived, I was hopeful for some real clarity about what we were supposed to be concentrating on so that we could bed-in and get on with things. Sadly, he really just left us to our own devices; got rid of Paul Travers, and then hit us with the commercial/industrial initiative. Mind you, he didn't load that all on us, which was fair. Although he wasn't what I would call a seasoned CEO, he was a superb salesman. Better than me, and I don't say that lightly. Seems to have been self-taught too. I was therefore surprised when he didn't transfer his skills and abilities into being CEO. He had all the jargon and he certainly looked the part, but there was something missing. Basically, he struggled to bring us with him; particularly Gilbert and Edith, although neither of them is easy.

Looking back, I think we needed more detail about what we were supposed to be doing. It's all very well looking at new markets, but I needed help with our *existing* markets; a proper sales strategy, which was never really forthcoming. I'm good on the road, and at managing my team and third-parties, but I'm not what you might call a strategist. With his background, I was hopeful that we could develop something, but in the end, he just focused on targets and I had to play the 'underpaid and undervalued' card, which wasn't what I was hoping for. I suppose it was partly my fault for not forcing the issue, but there's only so much you can do when the focus is revenue.

In retrospect, I think Toby's big mistake was focussing too much on growth and not enough on profit. He constantly repeated the mantra of 'profitable growth' as handed to him by the board, but in my view, profits were more important than growth for them. Once the money was there, there was going to be a lot more we could have done.

When I saw Toby being marched out of the building, I have to confess, I was shocked. I assumed, as did many of us, that he must have had his hand in the till or had been up to something dodgy. Turns out the board just lost faith in his ability to deliver something substantial. Couldn't work out where he was going beyond the big picture. I suppose it was the same for all of us. It will be interesting to see how this new bloke fares now.

Gilbert Turkey – Indirect Sales Manager

I know I can be a bit impulsive, but I think I'm a valuable member of the team, except when I see stupidity, arrogance, or someone tries to sideline or disrespect me. I can't stand people throwing their weight around, particularly if they don't know what they're talking about. I don't think I would have lasted with Hamish, even though I'm married to his daughter, if I'd behaved too badly. And in performance terms, I've always delivered enough leads to keep the business going. In fact, over the past few years, I've delivered enough to increase sales by a significant percentage. So I didn't take kindly to someone being parachuted in, and starting to challenge the work I was doing quite successfully.

Thinking back to Toby's introduction to the company, I have to say that I don't think it was handled particularly well. Unlike the rest of the SMT, I sneaked into the back of the town hall called by the chairman as I was curious about what was going on, and quite frankly it was a bit of a mess. Something as big as a new CEO needs a careful introduction and some preparation of the ground beforehand, but Toby was sprung on us without warning, and the chairman then proceeded to give some excuse about Hamish's health. Everyone knew Hamish had a drink problem, which I suppose is a health issue of sorts. However, I still think he could have provided a better explanation and given us some early signals. I knew there were some confidential discussions taking place; whenever I happened on a conversation between Hamish and the chairman, they always went silent. I'd not thought it was as serious as a resignation, but clearly something was afoot.

I don't recall Toby covering himself in glory at his introduction either. Well, not from my point of view anyway. After a general introduction, he then proceeded to trot out what I can only call business text-book platitudes, which he repeated at the first SMT when he formally introduced himself to the rest of the executives. I've done a few on-line business and management things, some from the CBI, others from the Chamber of Commerce, and I've read one or two books; and what I heard was straight off the page, so to speak. Well, you can imagine what I was thinking; bit of a 'fake sheik.' Authenticity is supposed to be one of the leadership traits required of good CEOs, so that really got up my nose.

I have to admit that I was not in a good frame of mind at that moment, as it was clear from the chairman's introduction that I had been overlooked as a candidate for the role. This was also clear when the chairman called the SMT together to make the announcement of Toby's appointment to us. The board knew that I would have liked to try my hand as CEO, so it was a bolt out of the blue and a bit of a snub to say the least. And then, of course, after all those fine words from Toby, none of them were followed by action. That was effectively the last we saw of Toby for quite some time, apart from our 1-2-1s, and mine did not go well. His so-called 'open door' stayed closed, and his interest in what we were doing seemed minimal.

After that, things went from bad to worse. We've never had budgets, and there he was demanding we create one and then stick to it. And then he wanted ROI figures for my work. I felt completely mistrusted, and there was no acknowledgement of what I'd been achieving for the business. And then I was basically excluded from any of the social media work that Toby had embarked on. Did he ask for any input? Not a sausage. And then later, he dumped the whole lot on me.

Now, as I said, I know I can be awkward, and that all stems from school. You can imagine how hard a time I had with a surname like Turkey. But if people listen to me, I can be quite good to work with. I know I can be pretty imaginative, and that I can be very clear about things when I can show that I'm correct. So when Toby introduced the idea of 'the original solar panel company,' without any backup evidence of why it was better, I was flabbergasted. I had similar reservations about leading with a 'green' positioning. I'm sure it has appeal, but does it generate enquiries? I'm still not sure about that.

My overall impressions? Well, not great as you may have gathered. Toby is clearly very experienced and probably a good salesperson. It's just that he seemed to be more concerned with playing a part than doing the job. When it came to strategic thinking, I'm not sure where he was. We had direction superficially, but so many people seemed a bit lost; they couldn't pin down exactly what they were supposed to do. Now that may say more about them than Toby, but I'd have said it was up to Toby to get whatever his message was over to them, and to make sure they understood what was required. Instead, we got what I call management mission speak, which made sense, but didn't really clarify anything.

Looks like I've now got to work with yet another outsider in Bob Meadows, but at least he seems to be able to listen, even if he can be a bit fierce. I know Edith has had her problems with him, but frankly, I think she is well past her sell-by-date.

Available worldwide from Amazon
and all good bookstores

Michael Terence
Publishing

www.mtp.agency

mtp.agency

@mtp_agency

Printed in Dunstable, United Kingdom

66044824R00109